Grammar Dimensions
Workbook Four

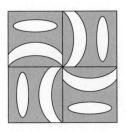

Gene Parulis

Jeff Williamson
**Northern Virginia
Community College**

**Heinle & Heinle Publishers
A Division of Wadsworth, Inc.
Boston, Massachusetts 02116 U.S.A.**

ISBN 0-8384-5147-0

10 9 8 7 6 5 4 3 2 1

Table of Contents

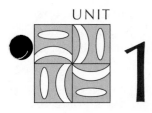

Verb Tenses in Discourse

Exercise 1 *(Focus 1)*

Underline the verbs of the main clauses in each sentence. Then state the time frame for each passage: present, past, or future. Circle words such as time adverbs that help to signal the time frame.

1. And then there is my cousin Bao-bao, whose real name is Roger. Everyone in the family has been calling him Bao-bao ever since he was a baby, which is what *bao-bao* means — "precious baby." Later, we kept calling him that because he was the crybaby who always wailed the minute my aunt and uncle walked in the door, claiming we other kids had been picking on him. And even though he's now thirty-one years old, we still think of him as Bao-bao — and we're still picking on him. (From *The Kitchen God's Wife* by Amy Tan. New York: Ballantine Books, 1991, p. 4.)

2. At thirty-four, I was the oldest student in the first-year class, perhaps in the whole school. And one of the least prepared as well. While nine-tenths of my classmates had been science majors, some even having completed advanced degrees and doctorates, I'd never been exposed to anything but literature and history years ago as an undergraduate at Princeton. Over the decade since then, I'd worked in semi-menial capacities in various hospitals and institutions, and it was only by going to night school for the past two years that I'd gained the bare minimum of credits in chemistry and physics and biology. With that kind of scanty and eccentric background, how could I survive? (From *Gentle Vengeance* by Charles LeBaron. New York: The Putnam Publishing Group, 1981.)

3. I'm shaking, trying to hold something inside. The last time I saw them, at the funeral, I had broken down and cried big gulping sobs. They must wonder now how someone like me can take my mother's place. A friend once told me that my mother and I were alike, that we had the same wispy hand gestures, the same girlish laugh, and the same sideways look. When I shyly told my mother this, she seemed insulted and said, "You don't even know little percent of me! How can you be me?" And she's right. How can I be my mother at Joy Luck? (From *The Joy Luck Club* by Amy Tan. New York: Ballantine Books, 1989, pp. 14–15.)

4. I did very well at the Academy. Throughout the four long winters I spent in Colorado Springs, there were few distractions and plenty of pressure to work harder, always work harder.

   Academy standards in the sciences and engineering were quite high. The rest of my courses, however, were more or less a matter of swallowing and regurgitating. This left plenty of time for the varsity track squad. At one point I was a quarter of the Academy's nationally ranked mile relay team. There was no time or inclination, of course, for thoughts on the growing anti-war movement except to note that the demonstrators looked hairy and dirty and were probably just lazy. Never mind. We Junior Birdmen would protect them from themselves. (From *Witness to War* by Charlie Clements. New York: Bantam Books, 1984, p. 65.)

5. After she finishes her A.S. degree in Computer Information Systems, Rosa is going to transfer to Iowa State University, where she will pursue a B.S. degree. She's going to room with her best friend Maria, who is studying Business Administration. Both of them will finish their degrees in two more years, and then they will take the summer off to see parts of the United States and Canada.

Exercise 2 *(Focus 2)*

Identify the moment or moments of focus for each passage. Discuss and determine whether each moment of focus is (1) a point of time or (2) a period of time, and whether it is explicitly stated or implied.

1. I've been working for the bus company for more than a year now. My mother was a ticket seller, too. She started working in 1958, during the Big Leap Forward. When she retired at the age of 50, I took over the job for her. In general now, the bus company doesn't recruit new workers from the outside. That's one way of providing jobs for the children of the people who work for the bus company. My father was a bus driver. He was born in Beijing and never left. (From *Chinese Profiles* by Zhang Xinxin and Sang Ye. Beijing: Chinese Literature Press, 1986, p. 113.)

2. There was this guy who used to ride the bus every day. He'd come up and start talking to me, even when I ignored him. This guy was really good looking. He told me he worked in a song and dance troupe. He even showed me his identity card. He really was an actor or something. But it never worked out. You never can trust the kind of people you meet on a bus. (From *Chinese Profiles* by Zhang Xinxin and Sang Ye. Beijing: Chinese Literature Press, 1986, p. 117.)

3. I thought, when I came as a student to Iowa, that I was coming simply to get a Master of Fine Arts degree in creative writing at the Writer's Workshop in the heartland. But now, thinking back on it, I realize that I was looking for more out of life; that I never really intended to go back to the very circumscribed, safe life that my parents had promised. While I was a student living in a dorm in Iowa City, Iowa, my parents did find for me the perfect Bengali groom for an arranged marriage. I didn't know the first name of this man. He had seen my photograph, and he'd said, "Terrific, I'll take her." I was expected, certainly, to do what girls of my class normally did—be happy in an arranged marriage; be content, anyway, in an arranged marriage. But deep down, I must have rejected that safe, circumscribed life. So fate sometimes is full of happy accidents, and I fell in love with a fellow student, Clark Blaise. After a two-week whirlwind courtship, we got married during lunchtime. And therefore, I made my life in this country. (From an interview with Bharati Mukherjee, in *Bill Moyers: A World of Ideas II*. New York: Doubleday, 1990, p. 7.)

4. All sixth graders in Hong Kong had to pass the Secondary School Entrance Exam before they could obtain a seat in secondary school. In 1964 when I took the exam, there were

more than twenty-thousand candidates. About seven thousand of us passed: four thousand were sent to government and subsidized schools, the other three thousand to private and grant-in-aid schools. I came in around no. 2000; I was lucky. Without the public exam, there would be no secondary school for So Tsi-fai. His future was sealed. (From "So Tsi-fai" by Sophronia Liu, in *Ourselves among Others,* Carol J. Verburg, editor. Boston: Bedford Books of St. Martin's Press, 1991, p. 219.)

Exercise 3 *(Focus 3)*

Each of the following passages has one sentence with an inappropriate verb tense for the context. Identify the sentence that has the error and correct it.

1. (a) The earth is the fifth largest planet and the third from the Sun. (b) It is the only planet in the solar system known to have water. (c) Its day, caused by its rotation, is between those of Neptune (16 hours) and Mars (24.5 hours). (d) Earth's seasons are caused by its tilt; when the North Pole of the planet is pointed toward the Sun, it will be summer in the Northern Hemisphere, and vice versa.

2. (a) The moon is larger than Pluto, the smallest planet in the solar system. (b) Its rotation takes exactly the same time as its orbit around the earth; thus it always shows the same side to the earth. (c) The moon wasn't solely responsible for raising and lowering the oceans of the earth, but its pull is 2.2 times greater than that of the Sun.

3. (a) Pluto's orbit is so irregular that it is now inside of Neptune's orbit. (b) Thus Pluto, until 1999, is the second farthest planet from the Sun. (c) Pluto took almost 248 Earth years to go around the Sun. (d) It rotates once every 6.4 days.

4. (a) Mercury is the second smallest planet in our solar system. (b) Because Mercury is so close to the Sun, its year takes only 88 Earth days. (c) However, Mercury rotates much more slowly than Earth, so a day on Mercury will take almost 59 Earth days; thus its year is less than two days long.

5. (a) Scientific projections of Mercury's surface temperature are very interesting. (b) The side closest to the Sun is estimated to be around 800°F (427°C) during the "day." (c) However, scientists do not agree on the temperature on the "night" side. (d) Some scientists believed that there is no atmosphere to regulate temperature, and thus the temperature plunges to −300°F (−184°C). (e) Some Russian scientists, however, believe that there is a regulating atmosphere, which holds the night side to "room temperature"— about 70°F (21°C).

6. (a) Mars is the third smallest planet, with a diameter about half the size of Earth. (b) A day on Mars will last almost exactly as long as a day on Earth—24 hours and 37 minutes. (c) A year, however, is about twice as long—687 days.

7. (a) Mariner 9, the first artificial satellite to be placed in an orbit about Mars, has photographed the entire planet's surface. (b) Preliminary study of these photos and other data shows that Mars resembles no other planet we know. (c) Some features of the planet's surface can be explained by volcanoes, earthquakes, craters, and glaciers, the last of which is no longer present on Mars. (d) Other features, including a canyon 10 times longer and three times deeper than the Grand Canyon, have been explained only with the premise that Mars once had large quantities of flowing water. (e) The exact composition

of the famous expanding and retracting caps on Mars' poles remains unknown, though most scientists believe them to be composed of both water and carbon dioxide ice.

8. (a) Predicting the movements of the planets was important to many past cultures, who believed that their fates were related to those of the planets. (b) Today many cultures still follow the movements of the planets and have paid special attention to their positions on important days such as births, deaths, and anniversaries.

9. (a) However, many physicists are unhappy with the continuing belief in the effect of the planets on people's lives. (b) Physicist and author Carl Sagan has noted that this effect is tested frequently in the case of twins. (c) Both will be born under identical planetary conditions, yet they can easily have very unequal fortunes.

10. (a) Still, the planets retained a special influence over our imagination. (b) Countless love poems deal with the moon and the planets—one of which, Venus, is considered to be the goddess of love. (c) And no pair of lovers can fail to appreciate the beauty of a full moon in a clear sky.

Exercise 4 *(Focus 4)*

Here are some passages from Studs Terkel's interviews in *The Great Divide* (see the textbook). Examine the passages and discuss both their overall time frames and their tense shifts. Use the questions below as a guide; more than one answer may be appropriate.

- Does the passage have a consistent overall time frame?
    - If so, is it present or past?
    - If not, what time frames does it have?
- What verb tenses do the speakers use to introduce topics?
- When speakers shift tenses, why do they do it?
    - To explain or support a general statement with past description, or elaborate on a topic.
    - To support a claim about the present with examples from the past.
    - To provide background information about a topic.
    - To express a comment or opinion about a topic.
    - To support a general statement about change by comparing past and present situations.

1. (a) I worry about the future every day. (b) Will we be able to put [our children] through college, if that's what they want? (c) Will they be out in the work force working for four dollars an hour? (d) What kind of home can you buy on four dollars an hour? (e) [My husband's] nephew, he's married, twenty-one, and working for four-fifty an hour.

2. (a) This year, nobody in the class asked me what I make. (b) They asked me questions about ethics: could they follow their own impulses if they worked on a newspaper? (c) I told them, on my job I'd just pick up on things that I thought people should know about. (d) I can't be an advocate working on a paper like the *Chicago Tribune,* but I can cover anti-apartheid protests on campuses and at least give them coverage. (e) I sensed

for the first time that kids were really interested in that stuff. (f) About six, seven years ago, it was always money. (g) I think it's changing.

3. (a) People are now shopping for churches. (b) In the old days, you went to the church where your parents and grandparents went. (c) And you expected your children to go. (d) There were expectations of a community. (e) You never thought of living with your boyfriend, because what would the community think? (f) They expected you would marry in their presence in the church. (g) Those expectations are gone because the community is gone. (h) The community is based on shared values.

4. (a) I'm forty-four, born two weeks after Pearl Harbor. (b) There was never any doubt I would go to college. (c) When I got married, I expected my children would go to college. (d) The possibility for that was lost in the divorce. (e) There isn't the money. (f) There's only so much you can do as a single parent. (g) And you're gone from the household during the day. (h) None of my three kids has gone to college.

5. (a) I was born in Dayton, Ohio. (b) My parents had come up from the South during the black migration. (c) They had met in the kitchen of the house where my mother was working as a domestic servant. (d) My father was working for a catering service. (e) It was during a party.

(f) There was always that upward-mobility feeling. (g) They did not have a lot of formal education, but they were definitely imbued with that Protestant work-ethic. (h) They were very religious and very family-oriented. (i) They were lower-income, they were not lower-class. (j) Those were the values they conveyed to me. (k) All the good old-fashioned values.

(l) I've often said that the first word I learned was not "mama," it was "college." (m) As far back as I can remember, it was understood that I was going to college.

6. (a) What concerns me is that I am so alone now. (b) There are so few blacks who have shared in this opportunity. (c) A few of us are allowed in the door and then it's shut. (d) No more. (e) I see a gap within our own community. (f) It reflects to some degree our society at large. (g) When the barriers of segregation finally fell, there was a massive rush, like a coiled spring finally unleashed. (h) Too many of our brothers and sisters were left behind. (i) That's what we're stuck with today.

7. (a) I decided I needed more training. (b) I joined a program in word processing, secretarial. (c) Since then, I've landed a real decent job as a paralegal. (d) I work with a lot of immigrants who are having a hard time.

Exercise 5 *(Focus 5)*   PAIR

Without reading the stories below, quickly choose story one, two, or three. Read the one you have chosen and memorize the basic story, and then close your book. Retell the story to your partner, using present tense verbs wherever possible to make the story seem more immediate. Then listen to your partner's story and decide if it seems more effective in the present tense.

1. A student took an exam in a large lecture course with over 300 students. At the end of the period, the professor announced that time was up, and the students had to turn in their exams. All the students came to the front and put their exams in a pile, except

for one student who remained at his seat for 10 extra minutes furiously filling in answers. When the student came to the front to hand in his exam, the professor told him that his grade would be lowered for taking too much time. Suddenly the student stiffened and indignantly asked the professor, "Do you know who I am?" The surprised professor replied, "No." The student replied, "Good!" and with one quick motion, lifted the huge pile of papers and placed his in the middle.

2. Four students sharing a dormitory room stayed out late one night and were too tired to get up in time for their early class the next morning. On the way to school, they all agreed on an excuse to tell the professor. They arrived near the end of class, and went up to the professor to ask if they could make up the day's quiz. The professor asked them why they were late, and they told him that it was because they had had a flat tire on the way to school. The professor told them to take their seats in separate corners of the room and each take out a sheet of paper for their quiz. He then asked them each to write down which tire was flat.

3. A woman was very unhappy. She had loaned a friend five hundred dollars, and she was worried because the friend never mentioned the loan and might try to deny it. Her father told her to write the friend a note, asking the friend for the one thousand dollars she had borrowed. The woman asked her father why she should say the amount was one thousand dollars. The father said that when the friend read the note, she would send another note stating that she only owed five hundred dollars, and then she couldn't deny the debt.

The story in number 4 is written in the present tense. Change the verbs to the past tense, and compare the two versions. Which do you like better? Why?

4. Three brothers are crossing a field together when a thunderstorm overtakes them. They run inside a half-ruined temple. The storm grows worse, and lightning begins to crash down in a great circle around the temple. The brothers are terrified, and they think that the lightning must be trying to strike one of them for being a sinner. So they decide to find out who it might be by hanging their hats outside of the temple door; whoever's hat is hit will have to leave the temple. They put the hats outside, and one of them is hit by a ferocious bolt of lightning. So they throw that farmer out into the storm. The lightning, however, stops for a moment, and then one final, enormous bolt smashes the temple and the men inside. For they are the real sinners for sending their brother out into the storm.

Verbs

Exercise 1 *(Focus 1)*

For each of the verbs underlined, decide which type of information is being conveyed by use of a simple or progressive tense, choose the letter of one or more of the categories given, and write it above the verb (refer to your textbook, Focus 1 and Focus 2, for examples). Multiple interpretations are possible; you may find it helpful to decide which types of information are *not* being conveyed.

Simple present expresses	Progressive aspect expresses
a. general ideas, relationships, and truths b. habitual or repeated actions c. mental perceptions or emotions d. possession or personal relationships e. time frame and moment of focus	f. actions already in progress at the moment of focus g. actions at the moment of focus as opposed to habitual actions h. repeated actions i. temporary situations in contrast to permanent states j. periods of time in contrast to points of time k. uncompleted actions

(1) <u>Are you wondering</u> how to get into the best companies or how to accelerate your rise to management? Many employers say they **(2)** <u>are looking for</u> people who **(3)** <u>have</u> an MBA degree in addition to their technical credentials.

Major firms often **(4)** <u>look</u> more closely at technical people with advanced management degrees. Some firms expressly **(5)** <u>ask</u> for upper-level degrees. According to one corporate recruiter, graduate management degree holders **(6)** <u>understand</u> not just how products are made, but also how corporations work.

Stephanie Tran **(7)** <u>believes</u> that her master's degree in Information Systems has helped her greatly. She **(8)** <u>feels</u> that the degree **(9)** <u>gives</u> her a view of how technology is used in business.

For example, Stephanie **(10)** <u>is currently writing</u> the specifications and instructions for a new system. Her technical knowledge **(11)** <u>provides</u> the detail the documentation needs. Her business knowledge **(12)** <u>helps</u> her understand the needs of the workers using the system. She **(13)** <u>is also looking</u> to the future for technical standards the company might want to adopt for future purchases, **(14)** <u>thinking</u> about future marketing applications, and **(15)** <u>building in</u> ways to cut costs.

Exercise 2 *(Focus 2)*

Decide whether a simple tense or progressive tense is appropriate for each blank and fill in the blank with the correct form of the verb in parentheses. Then choose one of the categories from Exercise 1 to explain *why* the verb is appropriate.

1. As she and her friends **(a)** _____ (talk) about the classes they

   (b) _____ (want) to take next semester, Lin **(c)** _____

   (notice) that Sang **(d)** _____ (seem) sad. When she **(e)** _____

   (ask) him what was wrong, he **(f)** _____ (tell) her that he

   (g) _____ (have) doubts about next semester. Although he

   (h) _____ (go) to school full-time last semester, he **(i)** _____

   (run) his sick father's business now, and he rarely **(j)** _____ (have)

   enough time to study.

2. Right now Tran **(a)** _____ (study) English at a community college.

   She **(b)** _____ (hope) to transfer to a four-year college and study

   electrical engineering. She **(c)** _____ (be) the first in her family to

   go to college, and so she **(d)** _____ (feel) a lot of pressure not

   to fail. She **(e)** _____ (have) very supportive parents, though, who

   (f) _____ (do, constantly) everything they can to

   encourage her. Her mother often **(g)** _____ (mail) her presents from

   home, and her father **(h)** _____ (tell, always) her how

   proud he **(i)** _____ (be) of her.

3. Kim **(a)** _____ (have) an R.N. degree, but she **(b)** _____

   (work) as a waitress until her English **(c)** _____ (improve) enough

   for her to pass her nursing exam. Every day she **(d)** _____ (work)

   from ten in the morning until late at night, sometimes one or two o'clock. She

   (e) _____ (be) so tired when she gets home that she just

   (f) _____ (take) a shower while her dinner **(g)** _____

   (cook), **(h)** _____ (eat) dinner, and **(i)** _____ (go) to

   bed without any time to study. She **(j)** _____ (realize) that her schedule

(k) _____ (take) away her opportunities to improve herself, but she really

(l) _____ (need) the money.

Exercise 3 (*Focus 3*)

Underline the present perfect and past perfect verbs in the following passages. Explain what information is expressed by the perfective aspect of these verbs. Choose one or more of the categories below (refer to Focus 3 in your textbook for examples).

We use perfect tenses to express the following:

- Events that happen before the moment of focus
- Events that began in the past and continue to be true at present in contrast to completed events
- Events that the speaker believes are relevant to the moment of focus in contrast to unrelated events

1. The day begins at 4:30 A.M. At that time I can hear Rosalie, the fifty-year-old woman who runs this little farm, padding to and fro in soft slippers doing I know not what to the stove, the dishes, the kitchen, and the pantry. By the time I get up, a couple of hours later, the cows have been attended to, breakfast prepared, the washing hung out, apples peeled, eggs collected, and other unseen tasks performed. Rosalie waves me to the kitchen table; and, though the gruel is curiously sour, I must eat, for she has made it especially for me and has filled it full of her best grains and buttermilk. She nods, smacks her lips, smiles her head, in vicarious delight, with every spoonful I take. I smile and grunt right back, and lately I have meant it, for the flavor of the stuff begins to grow on you. (From *Journal of a War: Northwest Europe, 1944–45* by Donald Pearce. The Macmillan Company of Canada, 1965.)

2. (a) My work alone had awarded me a top place and I was going to be one of the first called in the graduating ceremonies. On the classroom blackboard, as well as on the bulletin board in the auditorium, there were blue stars and white stars and red stars. No absences, no tardiness, and my academic work was among the best of the year.

    (b) My hair pleased me too. Gradually the black mass had lengthened and thickened, so that it kept at last to its braided pattern and I didn't have to yank my scalp off when I tried to comb it.

    (c) I hoped the memory of that morning would never leave me. Sunlight was itself young, and the day had none of the insistence maturity would bring it in a few hours. In my robe and barefoot in the backyard, under cover of going to see about my new beans,

I gave myself up to the gentle warmth and thanked God that no matter what evil I had done in my life He had allowed me to live to see this day. (From *I Know Why the Caged Bird Sings* by Maya Angelou. New York: Random House, Inc., 1969.)

3. In a theater the other day I saw a picture of a man who had developed the soap bubble to a higher point than it had ever before reached. He had become the ace soap bubble blower of America, had perfected the business of blowing bubbles, refined it, doubled it, squared it, and had even worked himself up into a convenient lather. The effect was not pretty. Some of the bubbles were too big to be beautiful, and the blower was always jumping into them or out of them, or playing some sort of unattractive trick with them. It was, if anything, a rather repulsive sight. Humor is a little like that: it won't stand much blowing up, and it won't stand much poking. It has a certain fragility, an evasiveness, which one had best respect. (From "Some Remarks on Humor" by E.B. White. From an adaptation to the preface to *A Subtreasury of American Humor*, edited by Katherine S. White and E.B. White. New York: Harper and Row, 1954.)

Exercise 4 *(Focus 3)*

Choose either a simple or perfect tense to fill in each blank. More than one answer may be correct; be prepared to explain why you chose one aspect. You may find the review of points below (from your textbook) helpful:

Simple tenses express	Perfective aspect expresses
a. general ideas, relationships, and truths b. habitual or repeated actions c. mental perceptions or emotions d. possession or personal relationships e. time frame and moment of focus	f. events that happen before the moment of focus g. events that began in the past and continue to be true at present in contrast to completed events h. events that the speaker believes are relevant to the moment of focus in contrast to unrelated events

For years many Americans **(1)** _____ (believe) that somewhere between the ages of 40 and 60 people **(2)** _____ (suffered) something called a "midlife crisis." This **(3)** _____ (be) the feeling that youth

(4) _____ (be) permanently behind, and only old age

(5) _____ (lie) ahead. The stereotypical response to a midlife crisis

(6) _____ (involve) some attempt to regain youth, and indeed, there

(7) _____ (be) many newspaper stories about women having plastic surgery and men having affairs with younger women.

However, some recent studies **(8)** _____ (place) doubt on this stereotype, particularly for people who **(9)** _____ (possess) certain traits. One research group **(10)** _____ (learn) that people who **(11)** _____ (be) happiest during their middle ages **(12)** _____ (look) honestly at themselves and **(13)** _____ (accept) the changes that **(14)** _____ (come) with age. At middle age, these people **(15)** _____ (understand) that they **(16)** _____ (have, not) the same strength or beauty as they **(17)** _____ (have) when they **(18)** _____ (be) twenty. So instead of relying on their physical qualities, at midlife these people **(19)** _____ (learn) to use the skills and wisdom the years **(20)** _____ (give) them. Often they use these qualities in ways that they **(21)** _____ (consider, not) before. Women especially **(22)** _____ (tend) to find surprising strengths in themselves at middle age. For example, the writers Kate Chopin and Edith Wharton **(23)** _____ (publish, not) anything before the age of 40.

Studies on relationships at middle age **(24)** _____ (find) a steady decline of stress in marriages all the way from youth into old age. Researchers **(25)** _____ (believe) that this **(26)** _____ (be) at least partly caused by what couples **(27)** _____ (learn) about each other when they are young. Finally, although in past studies middle-aged adults **(28)** _____ (score) lower than their younger counterparts on standardized cognitive tests, some researchers now **(29)** _____ (feel) that middle-aged people may simply see problems in equally intelligent but different ways from the young. Although they may not compute problems as quickly, middle-aged people **(30)** _____ (collect) more experience to base their solutions on. A young gardener might make a wonderful plan for his garden from the best books available, only to see his older neighbor's plot prosper from his greater knowledge of the weather and soil in that area.

Exercise 5 *(Focus 3)*

The perfective aspect is used to express (A) events that happen before the moment of focus, (B) events that begin in the past and continue to be true at present in contrast to completed events, and (C) events that the speaker believes are relevant to the moment of focus in contrast to unrelated events. Underline the perfect verbs in the following passages, and decide what type(s) of information are being expressed by the perfective aspect of these verbs. The first one has been done for you as an example.

1. (a) There was, however, one Italian import whose vocabulary <u>has had</u> an influence on the language out of all proportion to its significance in the American-Italian community: the Mafia. (b) Now treated as synonymous with organized crime (which it is not), the Mafia has added terms like *godfather, the family,* and *capo* to the language. (c) Hollywood's love affair with "gangster movies" has ensured a wide dissemination of criminal slang: *hoodlum, racketeer, rough house, hatchet man, doing the dirty work, hot seat* (originally "the electric chair"), *protection racket* and *loan shark.* (From *The Story of English* by Robert McCrum, William Cran, and Robert MacNeil. New York: Viking, 1986.)

2. (a) It is always tempting to make a direct link between the play of the child and the work of the adult . . . (b) None other than Frank Lloyd Wright himself recounted in his autobiography that he had played with Froebel blocks and that these had had an important influence on his creative development. (c) The Los Angeles architect Frank Gehry has claimed that his choice of career was influenced by his childhood construction play, and several of his projects do have the air of large playthings. (d) As a young graduate I worked for Moshe Safdie, the architect of Montreal's Habitat, which has often been likened to a pile of children's blocks and was in fact designed using Lego bricks. (From *The Most Beautiful House in the World* by Witold Rybczynski. New York: Viking, 1989.)

3. (a) The hallmark of the United States has been growth. (b) Americans have typically defined this process in quantitative terms. (c) Never was that more true than in the first half of the nineteenth century, when an unparalleled rate of growth took place in three dimensions: population, territory, and economy. (d) In 1850, Zachary Taylor—the last president born before the Constitution—could look back at vast changes during his adult life. (e) The population of the United States had doubled and then doubled again. (f) Pushing relentlessly westward and southward, Americans had similarly quadrupled the size of their country by settling, conquering, annexing, or purchasing territory that had been occupied for millennia by Indians and claimed by France, Spain, Britain, and Mexico. (From *Battle Cry of Freedom: The Civil War Era* by James M. McPherson. New York: Oxford University Press, 1988).

4. (a) The summer of 1863 was one of the hardest for Richmonders, who were by then enduring the worst that the war has to visit upon a people. (b) Hospitals were jammed . . . and deaths were numerous. (c) The preceding summer there had been a flicker of hope, when General Lee had routed McClellan's forces from the . . . city, but the cruel winter . . . had taken its toll by the spring of 1863. (d) On 2 April there occurred an event still referred to as the "Bread Riot." (e) Because speculators had made the situation worse by greatly inflating prices, city residents were running out of food. (f) Accordingly, a group of desperate women met at the Belvidere Baptist Church on Oregon Hill and began a march to the capitol, a distance of over a mile. (From *A Richmond Reader: 1733–1983,* edited by Maurice Duke. Chapel Hill, N.C.: University of North Carolina Press, 1983.)

Exercise 6 *(Focus 3)*

Decide whether you should use a simple future or future perfect tense of each verb in parentheses to fill in the blank.

College students **(1)** _____ (have) to compare the value of their degree with the time that **(2)** _____ (be) needed to obtain it. A medical student, for example, might say to herself, "When I graduate, I **(3)** _____ (be) 28 years old and **(4)** _____ (go) to college for over 12 years. I **(5)** _____ (spend) more than $60,000 on my education and **(6)** _____ (have) most of that amount in loans. **(7)** _____ (be, I) satisfied with my profession enough to justify these expenditures?" Some students feel that school alone **(8)** _____ (guarantee, not) their security or happiness; they worry that the job market **(9)** _____ (change) by the time they graduate, or that they **(10)** _____ (have, not) enough work experience to compete for the best jobs, or that they **(11)** _____ (spend) a lot of time and money on their degree only to learn that they aren't satisfied with their career when they finally get a job. Therefore more and more students are choosing to study part-time while they work or to include cooperative education in their degree programs, so they can gain more job experience and a greater understanding of just what their careers **(12)** _____ (be) like.

Exercise 7 *(Focus 3)*

Imagine that you are a bank personnel manager who has to interview an applicant for the bank's armored car (money truck) fleet. Write down five questions you would ask about the applicant's skills, and, since this is a position of high responsibility, three questions you would ask about the applicant's background to see if the applicant can be trusted. Examine and explain the tense/aspect choice that you made.

Applicant's skills:

1. _____?
2. _____?
3. _____?
4. _____?
5. _____?

Applicant's background:

1. _____?
2. _____?
3. _____?

Below is a badge given to many people on election day after they vote. Why do you think that the question on the bottom is put in the present perfect?

I voted
have you?

_____

_____

_____

_____

_____

Exercise 8 *(Focus 4)*

Decide whether the verbs in parentheses should express an action, event, or situation completed at a specific time in the past (simple past) or one that started in the past and continues to the present (present perfect or present perfect progressive). Write the appropriate form for each verb in the blank. More than one verb form may be appropriate for some blanks.

For a long time, Lois **(1)** _____ (work) on nights and on weekends. For the past three years, she and her husband Omar **(2)** _____ (try) to save enough money to buy a house. Interest rates **(3)** _____ (go) down for the past few months, so Lois and Omar think that now is a good time to buy. They **(4)** _____ (look) at houses in the city, but decided that a house in the suburbs would be considerably cheaper. Lately they **(5)** _____ (talk) to an agent about a house with a big yard near Lois's mother. Their real-estate agent **(6)** _____ (plan) to sell the house to another couple, but the couple changed their minds and so now Lois and Omar have a chance.

Exercise 9 *(Focus 5)*

Choose simple present, present progressive, present perfect, or present perfect progressive for each blank. More than one answer could be correct; be prepared to explain your choices.

Li Hong **(1)** _____ (feel) that her friends and her family **(2)** _____ (be) her two most important in-groups. She **(3)** _____ (be) close to about five friends for a long time. All of them **(4)** _____ (be) in the United States now, where two **(5)** _____ (study) nursing, and three **(6)** _____ (study) computer information systems. They **(7)** _____ (go) to three different schools in California, Virginia, and New York. They still **(8)** _____ (keep) in close contact with each other, though. In fact, Li Hong even **(9)** _____ (complain) a little about Yi Mei, who always **(10)** _____ (call) her up late at night while she **(11)** _____ (try) to study. For two years now, the friends **(12)** _____ (come) to Li Hong's house for Chinese New Year, since all their families **(13)** _____ (still, live) in Taiwan.

   Li Hong's family **(14)** _____ (support) her both financially and emotionally during her stay in the United States. Her father often **(15)** _____ (send) her money and little letters of encouragement, while her mother frequently **(16)** _____ (mail) her small packages of food and **(17)** _____ (visit) her twice in the past two years. Li Hong especially **(18)** _____ (treasure) her family's long phone calls. Because some of her friends **(19)** _____ (be) originally from China, Li Hong **(20)** _____ (have) to speak Mandarin Chinese with them. However, when her family **(21)** _____ (call), she can use the Taiwan dialect, which has a lot of happy memories for her.

Exercise 10 *(Focus 6)*

Fill in the blanks on the next page with simple present, simple past, past progressive, past perfect, or past perfect progressive forms of the verbs given. More than one answer may be correct; be prepared to explain your choice.

Many people **(1)** _____ (think) of dragons and heroes and monsters in the woods when they **(2)** _____ (hear) the word "legend." But there **(3)** _____ (be) other types of legends. Did you ever hear about the woman who **(4)** _____ (try) to dry her poodle in a microwave when the dog **(5)** _____ (explode)? Or the mysterious child hitchhiker that **(6)** _____ (appear) on a piece of road where a child **(7)** _____ (kill) years earlier? If you **(8)** _____ (hear) any of these or other stories that just **(9)** _____ (sound) a little *too* interesting, you likely **(10)** _____ (hear) an urban legend.

American college campuses **(11)** _____ (host) a number of persistent urban legends over the years. Like legends from faraway places, these urban legends often **(12)** _____ (deal) with fantastic, grotesque, and odd occurences. One famous legend **(13)** _____ (be) that the administration will give a student straight A's if his or her roommate **(14)** _____ (commit) suicide. Other legends **(15)** _____ (concern) hidden lives of faculty members, such as the professor who **(16)** _____ (invent) a chemical warfare agent but **(17)** _____ (be) now prohibited from discussing it.

College students also **(18)** _____ (appear) in more common myths, such as the student on vacation who **(19)** _____ (drinking) and **(20)** _____ (wake) up the next day to find a scar on his back where his kidney **(21)** _____ (be). Another legend **(22)** _____ (concern) a student who **(23)** _____ (buy) a sports car from a woman for fifty dollars. The woman's husband **(24)** _____ (run) away with

16

another woman, and later **(25)** _____ (write) his wife, instructing her to sell his beloved sports car for whatever she could.

Interestingly, some urban legends **(26)** _____ (acquire) international status. Until recently, an Internet discussion group **(27)** _____ (look) at urban legends from around the world. One story **(28)** _____ (concern) a little boy who **(29)** _____ (die) of some illness, and **(30)** _____ (need) to collect a huge number (say, 10,000) of one essentially worthless item (such as bottle caps or business cards) to purchase an iron lung or other such piece of medical equipment. Confirmations of this legend **(31)** _____ (come) from New Zealand, the United Kingdom, Israel, and Norway, among other places.

Subject-Verb Agreement

Exercise 1 *(Focus 1)*

For each sentence below, identify the subject and circle its head noun. Then complete the sentence with a correct form of the verb.

E X A M P L E : The reading (habits) of a group *give* (give) some measure of its intellectual activity.

The survey of American reading habits in your textbook **(1)** _____ (be) interesting. Most Americans these days probably **(2)** _____ (believe) that fewer, not more, people read regularly. One of the reasons for this belief in declining reading habits **(3)** _____ (be) the explosion of the amount of television available. Cable-TV subscribers in an area like New York City **(4)** _____ (receive) more than 100 channels.

Another piece of evidence that Americans read less **(5)** _____ (be) the well-documented fall in U.S. student test scores, particularly in comparison to student scores in other countries, such as Japan. However, some studies of student time use **(6)** _____ (have) shown that average Japanese students actually watch *more* TV than their American counterparts. Their success in part **(7)** _____ (come) from also doing more homework than American students.

Some prominent writers such as Camille Paglia **(8)** _____ (have) argued that reading books **(9)** _____ (be) an outdated skill in this age of electronic media. Media critic Neil Postman, on the other hand, **(10)** _____ (have) argued that reading books **(11)** _____ (remain) a uniquely rewarding and necessary activity.

A quick look at their books **(12)** _____ (leave) one a little confused. Paglia's book *Sexual Personnae* **(13)** _____ (be) 736 pages long, while Postman's books **(14)** _____ (have) tended to be less than 200 pages each.

Exercise 2 (Focus 2)

First, put brackets around any modifying phrases following the head noun. Next, identify the subject of the sentences below and circle its head noun. Finally, fill in the blank with the verb given.

EXAMPLE: The Library of Congress catalog system, which most U.S. libraries use, *classifies* (classify) books as either "fiction" or "nonfiction."

The kind of fiction that each person likes to read **(1)** _____ (be) a matter of individual taste. The four most popular writers in the Gallup survey discussed in the textbook **(2)** _____ (write) in a variety of genres.

One thing that most of the favorite books have in common **(3)** _____ (be) their designation as "popular," or mass-market, reading. This designation, which is made frequently by booksellers and reviewers, **(4)** _____ (be) hard to define. Generally speaking, a book that is unpopular with critics **(5)** _____ (be) considered "popular." Supposedly, this kind of book, compared to books typically taught in college literature courses, **(6)** _____ (have) less depth of thought.

However, a review of books considered "popular" over the years **(7)** _____ (show) that the designation can change. Charles Dickens, along with a number of other Victorian writers, **(8)** _____ (be) enormously popular with readers in his time, yet his works are studied widely in college literature courses. Even Shakespeare's plays, widely considered the paradigm of thoughtful literature in English, **(9)** _____ (be) listed as "works of diversion" for students in an eighteenth-century catalog at Yale University.

Whatever they are reading, readers inevitably find certain conditions that improve their reading. Some people **(10)** _____ (find) that eyeglasses, as opposed to contacts, **(11)** _____ (help) their reading. Others might prefer a special place or a cup of coffee. It is clear that desire, not any innate abilities, **(12)** _____ (make) an avid reader.

Exercise 3 (Focus 3)

Fill in the blank with a form of the verb given. In some cases you may have to make additional choices in singular/plural agreement.

EXAMPLE: Both *The Joy Luck Club* and *The Kitchen God's Wife* <u>were</u> (be) best-sellers for author Amy Tan.

Although both Sue Grafton and Elmore Leonard **(1)** _____ (write)

mystery novels, **(2)** _____ (his/her/their) styles are quite different.

Despite the fact that neither Ralph Ellison nor Mary Shelley

(3) _____ (have) written more than a few books, both Ellison and

Shelley **(4)** _____ (be) regarded as **(5)** _____

(a major writer/major writers). On the other hand, both Danielle Steele and Louis L'Amour

(6) _____ (have) written numerous best-sellers without being given

much critical attention.

Neither Ray Bradbury nor most other science fiction authors **(7)** _____

(appeal) much to Takako. She says that either nonfiction books, such as histories and

biographies, or a realistic fiction writer like James Clavell **(8)** _____

(interest) her.

(9) _____ (have) either Wan-shan or the other Chinese

students read *Iron and Silk* yet? Both that book and the movie of the same name

(10) _____ (tell) the story of Mark Salzman, an American English

teacher in China.

(11) _____ (do) either horror novels or a good suspenseful story ap-

peal to you? If so, either Stephen King or V.C. Andrews **(12)** _____ (be)

(13) _____ (a good choice/good choices) for you.

If neither the espionage novels of John LeCarre nor a book like *Red Storm Rising*

(14) _____ (appeal) to you, neither a writer like Tom Clancy nor books

like *Day of the Jackal* **(15)** _____ (be) **(16)** _____

(a good choice/good choices). Both Tom Clancy and Danielle Steele frequently

(17) _____ (find) **(18)** _____ (his/her/their)

(19) _____ (book/books) at the top of best-seller lists.

Exercise 4 *(Focus 4)*

Fill in the blank with a present tense form of the verb given. In some cases, you also need to
choose a singular or plural form of a given pronoun. The first one has been done for you as
an example.

Yassir's ESL class **(1)** *doesn't have* (have, not) a textbook. Instead, **(2)** _____
(they, it) **(3)** _____ (use) four novels. This method of teaching

(4) _____ (be) called "whole-language instruction." In this method, students are required to do large amounts of non-ESL reading and to respond to their reading in journals, which are read in groups. Vocabulary **(5)** _____ (be) improved by students selecting words to learn from the reading.

Right now Yassir's group **(6)** _____ (write) in **(7)** _____ (their/its) journals. The assignment **(8)** _____ (be) for students to write on how they felt about this method. Some people **(9)** _____ (like) it a lot. They feel that the additional information that **(10)** _____ (come) from the additional reading **(11)** _____ (help) them to understand native speakers better. Other people **(12)** _____ (like) the method less; they feel that the homework **(13)** _____ (be) too time-consuming.

Yassir's group **(14)** _____ (have) some good ideas. Research **(15)** _____ (favor, not) any single method of language teaching; rather, education—using any method—that **(16)** _____ (interest) students **(17)** _____ (be) the kind that will be successful. The interested **(18)** _____ (tend) to do well, while the disinterested **(19)** _____ (tend) to do poorly.

Exercise 5 *(Focus 5)*

Each of the sentences below requires two answers: a multiple choice answer and a fill-in-the-blank answer. The multiple choice part of each sentence, provided solely for your interest, requires a response to an information question. The fill-in-the-blank part of each sentence requires you to practice the verb forms that you studied in Focus 5. In all cases, the verb form is the same regardless of the information answer.

E X A M P L E : (ⓐ b c) *equals* one mile.

    a.   5,280 feet

    b.   10,000 feet

    c.   1,600 yards

1.   (a b c) per hour _____ (be) the speed limit on unmarked rural roads in the United States.

    a.   40 miles

    b.   55 miles

    c.   70 miles

2. (a b c) _____ (be) the study of bugs.
    a. Etymology
    b. Entomology
    c. Insectology

3. (a b c) _____ (be) necessary equipment for an ornithologist.
    a. A pair of binoculars
    b. A pair of suspenders
    c. A pair of pliers

4. (a b c) _____ (be) a deadly sexually transmitted disease that can be cured with penicillin.
    a. Syphilis
    b. AIDS
    c. Herpes

5. (a b c) _____ (be) the medical field concerned with illnesses that afflict the elderly.
    a. Orthopedics
    b. Geriatrics
    c. Obstetrics

6. (a b c) _____ (be) first stated by the astronomer Ptolemy.
    a. That the earth is the center of the universe
    b. That the sun is the center of the universe
    c. That the planets are held in place by gravity

7. (a b c) _____ (be) located west of Portugal.
    a. The Azores
    b. The Lesser Antilles
    c. The Kuril Islands

8. (a b c) _____ (be) the work of astrologers.
    a. Predicting the weather
    b. Studying the physical properties of heavenly bodies
    c. Predicting the influence of the stars on people's lives

9. (a b c) _____ (be) caused by moving too quickly from a high to a low atmospheric pressure.
    a. The bends
    b. The cramps
    c. The spasms

10. Complete the following line from Shakespeare's *Hamlet:*

    "(a b c); that _____ (be) the question."

    a. To love or not to love
    b. To be or not to be
    c. To live or not to live

11. (a b c) _____ (be) bordered by the Mississippi river.

    a. Texas
    b. Kansas
    c. Arkansas

12. In geometry, the sum of a closed figure's angles _____ (equals) (a b c).

    a. the number of sides minus two times 180 degrees
    b. the number of sides times 180 degrees
    c. the number of sides divided by two times 180 degrees

13. (a b c) _____ (be) useful at a barbecue.

    a. Tweezers
    b. Tongs
    c. Forceps

14. Before Pheidippides died in Athens from his 26-mile-long run, he delivered news that _____ (be) pleasing to his generals: (a b c).

    a. The Persians had won the battle of Marathon
    b. The Greeks had won the battle of Marathon
    c. Helen had been taken prisoner

15. Astronomical (a b c) _____ (are) often used to scan wide sections of sky before aiming a telescope.

    a. forceps
    b. spyglasses
    c. binoculars

16. *Hard Times* _____ (be) written by (a b c).

    a. Chaucer
    b. Dickens
    c. Scott

Exercise 6 (Focus 6)

Fill in the blank with the correct form of the verb given in parentheses.

E X A M P L E :   Although events in her life are similar to events in her books, all of Amy Tan's best-known work _is_ (be) fictional.

Six of the 15 best-selling hardcover children's books of all time **(1)** _____ (be) written by Dr. Seuss—the pen-name of Theodore Geizel.

One-third of the paperback list **(2)** _____ (be) filled with titles by Laura Ingalls Wilder. A lot of her work **(3)** _____ (deal) with pioneer children in the American midwest in the nineteenth century. A number of her books **(4)** _____ (be) the basis for a popular American TV program, _Little House on the Prairie._

Among adults, nearly everything V.C. Andrews wrote **(5)** _____ (have) sold well. Although Andrews' books have been written by another writer since her death, a lot of her audience **(6)** _____ (know) this, and none of them **(7)** _____ (seem) to mind.

His fans quickly buy almost every book Stephen King **(8)** _____ (have) written. Each of his books **(9)** _____ (have) been a best-seller.

Every year, although a number of new information almanacs **(10)** _____ (be) written, the number of _World Almanacs_ sold still **(11)** _____ (continue) to climb.

Nora felt that none of the clerk's advice **(12)** _____ (be) useful as she perused the books in the store. None of them **(13)** _____ (be) what she was looking for for her father. Her father always made sure that everyone in the family **(14)** _____ (be) an avid reader. Therefore, they already had a lot of titles at home.

Exercise 7 (Focus 7)

Fill in the blank with the correct form of the verb given.

E X A M P L E :   A small but unified minority _is_ (be) helping mayoral candidate Wilson to the top in voter opinion polls.

A small but vocal minority **(1)** _____ (have) objected to the inclusion of some well-known books in school libraries. The majority of the complaints

(2) _____ (have) centered around racial or sexual themes in the books. Although a 90-percent majority of parents surveyed **(3)** _____ (be) opposed to the removal of the problem books, in most cases, the complainants were given a public hearing. Typically, only a minority of the books in question **(4)** _____ (reveal) sustained prejudicial views of the authors. Rather, the offending passages are usually related to prejudiced characters whom the author condemns.

A sizeable majority **(5)** _____ (feel) that the right to free speech is more important than the right to be free from offensive speech. Therefore, these kinds of protests are rarely successful. And although they make good news stories, only a tiny minority of school districts—less than 1 percent nationwide—ever **(6)** _____ (face) this problem.

Exercise 8 *(Focus 8)*

Jack and Robert are fishing together. Jack is a very informal person, while Robert is scrupulously formal. Fill in the blanks of their conversation with the correct form of **be** according to the formal and informal rules you studied in Focus 8 in your textbook. The first one has been done for you as an example.

Robert: Could you please hand me a soft drink from the cooler?

Jack: **(1)** *There's* two colas and two ginger ales—which do you want?

Robert: Either of them **(2)** _____ fine.

Jack: Hold on a second—neither of the colas **(3)** _____ cold. And one of the ginger ales is a diet ginger ale. Which do you want?

Robert: Either the colas or the regular ginger ale **(4)** _____ fine. Oh, there **(5)** _____ some clean drinking cups as well, right?

Jack: Uh, no. There **(6)** _____ some cups, but none of them **(7)** _____ clean. What's wrong with drinking from the can?

Robert: Neither your dirty hands nor the can **(8)** _____ free of the sorts of germs that could ruin a perfectly splendid fishing trip.

Jack: Well, either your complaints or my headache **(9)** _____ ruining my trip.

Robert: You needn't be so rude. Neither you nor I **(10)** _____ here to do anything but enjoy ourselves.

Jack: Which, I might add, neither you nor I **(11)** _____ doing as long as we're arguing instead of fishing.

Choose the <u>one</u> word or phrase that best completes the sentence.

1. Nguyet said that either her mother or her brothers _____ come with her to the picnic.
   - (A) plan to
   - (B) is planning to
   - (C) plans to
   - (D) has plans to

2. Every one of the workers _____ with the new agreement.
   - (A) is pleased
   - (B) are pleased
   - (C) have been pleased
   - (D) were pleased

3. It seemed so nice when we looked at it in June. The carpet _____ installed and the windows overlooked the park.
   - (A) has just been
   - (B) had just been
   - (C) is just
   - (D) will have just been

4. An overwhelming majority _____ the president's plan.
   - (A) does not support
   - (B) are not going to support
   - (C) do not support
   - (D) were not in support of

5. Angela usually works in the marketing division, but she _____ in sales until Melissa gets out of the hospital.
   - (A) works
   - (B) has worked
   - (C) worked
   - (D) is working

6. Two-thirds of what the president said _____ true.
   - (A) were
   - (B) was
   - (C) are
   - (D) seem

7. When the fight broke out, David _____ to Grace.
   - (A) talked
   - (B) will speak with
   - (C) has been talking
   - (D) was talking

8. Counting today, Maria _____ absent from class for four consecutive days.
   - (A) is
   - (B) was
   - (C) has been
   - (D) will be

9. As a result of better engineering, fatality rates from car accidents _____ for the past ten years.
   (A) are declining   (C) decline
   (B) have declined   (D) were declining

10. We will not renew our lease in August. Instead, we _____ a house with some friends.
    (A) rent   (C) can rent
    (B) will rent   (D) planned to rent

11. The committee _____ with the project for weeks before the chairman cut their funding.
    (A) had been struggling   (C) struggles
    (B) has been struggling   (D) has struggled

12. Our new apartment is awful. The heater doesn't work, the sink leaks, and the refrigerator _____ a fuse every time it comes on.
    (A) will blow   (C) blows
    (B) has blown   (D) blew

13. In my essay, I said that the main reason I came to this college _____ its excellent research facilities.
    (A) are   (C) is
    (B) have been   (D) were

14. By the year 2020, world population _____ to 8.2 billion people.
    (A) increases   (C) has increased
    (B) will have increased (D) increased

15. The binoculars I received for Christmas _____ excellent for bird-watching.
    (A) am   (C) are
    (B) is   (D) was

Identify the one underlined word or phrase that must be changed in order for the sentence to be grammatically correct.

16. Jefferson High School's principal, not the parents, want to extend the school year, but
                                               A

    the students at the school say that their teachers give enough work already, and they
                             B   **C**

    need the summer to recover for the next year.
    D

17. Neither the workers nor the owner feel that their present contract is acceptable, so they
    _____A   ____B
    have decided to hire a negotiator to help them reach an agreement.
    ____C   ____D

18. At the meeting tonight, the mayor will explain what she wants from the police depart-
                                   _____A   _____B
    ment, and the police is going to explain everything they have asked the mayor for.
                         _____C   _____D

19. At a transportation conference we went to, a freight company manager said that eight
                                      ____A   ____B
    hours driving were not enough for his drivers to deliver goods, so they often drove
                 ____C   _____D
    illegal overtime hours.

20. One of the teachers complained that more than three-fourths of her preparation time
                       _____A
    were spent on evaluation, while she felt that she needed more time to prepare lectures
    ____B   ____C   _____D
    and class activities.

21. After Masha was injured in the game, the coach said that although he hoped that her
                _____A   ____B
    health were going to improve, he was going to remove her from the team so that another
         ____C   _____D
    player could have a chance.

22. My brother-in-law recently had bought a house—he has been studying the mortgage
                              _____A   _____B
    rates, and feels that now is a good time to buy.
             ____C   __D

23. The landlord says he will send someone to fix the heater next week, but we won't
               ____A   _____B   _____C   _____D
    believe him.

24. Because he has been feeling tired and wants a change in his life, James has taken a
                _____A   _____B   _____C
    temporary leave of absence from his job and does work with retarded children this
                                            ____D
    summer.

25. Shazia is planning to visit Acapulco this winter; her mother just returned from there,
           _____A   _____B
    and had told Jane how much she enjoyed her vacation.
        _____C   _____D

26. Jonas is looking at several possible medical schools that he thinks will be good choices
           _____A   _____B ____C
    for him after he will graduate in May.
                  _____D

27. We were working on our assignment for three hours when a student ran into the lab
       _____A   ___B
    and said that there was a fire.
        ___C   ____D

28. Mary has written to several publishers about the book that she just finished, and now
          _____A   _____B
    waits to see if any of them will publish it.
    ___C   _____D

28

Perfective Modals

Exercise 1 *(Focus 1)*

Part A: Fill in the blanks with the active voice of the perfective modals given. Marcia and Juan decided to stop seeing each other. Both of them have been thinking about the reasons their relationship went bad.

E X A M P L E : Marcia wonders if she *could have treated* (could, treat) Juan better.

Marcia thinks she **(1)** _____ (could, be) nicer to Juan when he forgot her birthday; Juan thinks he often **(2)** _____ (may, spend) too much time with his friends instead of Marcia. Marcia feels that she **(3)** _____ (should, not, expect) Juan to know how hurt she was about the birthday incident without telling him so; Juan knows that he **(4)** _____ (should, not, hang up) the phone on Marcia when they got into their last argument. Both of them feel that they **(5)** _____ (could, do) a lot of things differently to improve their relationship.

Part B: Fill in the blanks with the passive form of the perfective modals given.

E X A M P L E : Juan knows that some things *should have been left* (should, leave) unsaid.

Marcia's brother agreed that their last argument **(6)** _____ (could, handle) better; Juan's sister told him that she **(7)** _____ (should, told) about the problems they were having. Marcia feels that there **(8)** _____ (might, not, be) so many problems between them if they had only talked more; Juan feels that there were a lot of things that **(9)** _____ (should, not, say). Both of them feel that their problems **(10)** _____ (could, avoid) if they had seen them more clearly.

Part C: Fill in the blanks with the perfective modal and present participle form of the verb given.

E X A M P L E : Marcia thinks that Juan *must have been dreaming* (must, dream) when he asked if they could still be friends.

Marcia wonders what she **(11)** _____ (must, thinking) when she told Juan she hated him. Juan wonders what on Earth he **(12)** _____ (could, hope for) when he tried to make things better by coming to talk to Marcia at 2 A.M. Both of them feel that they **(13)** _____ (should, pay) more attention to each other instead of worrying about other things.

Exercise 2 *(Focus 2)*

In your textbook, review the meanings expressed by the modals **should have**, **could have**, and **might have**. Then, for the exercises below, underline the meaning-word clues for each sentence and fill in the blank with an appropriate modal. Several answers are possible for some blanks.

E X A M P L E : I underline regret that I yelled at you. I *should have* been nicer.

Marcia was really irritated when Juan said that their problems were all her fault. She felt that he **(1)** _____ accepted some of the blame.

Juan felt that Marcia **(2)** _____ done a lot to help a friend of his who worked with her. It was well within her abilities as office manager to prevent him from getting fired, and give him a second chance.

Marcia thought it was really thoughtless of Juan to volunteer to work overtime on Christmas eve. He **(3)** _____ worked overtime any other night of the year.

Juan told Marcia that he really regretted some of his actions, and that he **(4)** _____ been more thoughtful.

Marcia was really angry at Juan when he showed up an hour late for a dinner date. She felt that he **(5)** _____ at least called.

Juan thought Marcia made a really rude comment to his sister about her prom dress. Marcia **(6)** _____ had the decency to keep her thoughts to herself.

Despite his protests that he had an exam the next week, Marcia felt that Juan was perfectly able to come and help her move into her new apartment last month, and that he **(7)** _____ at least helped with some of the heavy items.

Juan strongly criticized Marcia for saying that she wasn't feeling well one evening when she later went out with friends. She **(8)** _____ told him the truth.

Marcia reproached Juan for the same offense, saying that he **(9)** _____ considered the time that he said he had to work overtime, but went fishing instead.

Both of them know that they did some pretty thoughtless things, and

(10) _____ thought before they acted.

Exercise 3 *(Focus 3)*

Betty and Elizabeth are roommates. Betty is always informal, Elizabeth is always formal. Fill in their conversation below with the correct form of either **be supposed to have** or **be to have**.

Elizabeth: You know that we **(1)** _____ finished our group projects by next Tuesday. The instructor expects to have them graded by Thursday.

Betty: I thought we **(2)** _____ turned them in by last Friday. No matter, I didn't turn in anything, anyway.

Elizabeth: No, our bibliographies **(3)** _____ turned in by then, but school was closed because of the snow.

Betty: Oh. Well, when **(4)** _____ completed our term papers? By the end of school?

Elizabeth: No, silly. We **(5)** _____ them done two weeks before the end. You'd better get busy!

Exercise 4 *(Focus 4)*

Fill in the blanks with *must have, can't have, should have,* and *would have.*

Mahmoud: Uh-oh, the clock on the wall in the computer lab is four hours behind. The power **(1)** _____ gone off during the night.

Najat: Oh, dear—I hope our project wasn't lost. Hakim was working on it last night. He's a pretty conscientious programmer; he **(2)** _____ made backup copies while he was working. Let's check the directory and see.

Mahmoud: Uh-oh—there's nothing here. The power **(3)** _____ gone off before he backed anything up.

Najat: That **(4)** _____ happened! I set the backup time for five minutes—the machine **(5)** _____ at least made some kind of copy. Look at that big file on the bottom left of the directory.

Mahmoud: Hey, that's it! That's great, Najat. Listen, we **(6)** _____ lost everything if you had not thought to do that.

Exercise 5 (Focus 5)

One of the tasks of an attorney in court is to weaken opposing witnesses' testimony by inducing uncertainty wherever possible. One way to do this is by asking questions expressing uncertainty or possibility, as opposed to certainty. Read the dialogue below and write in the missing questions. The first one has been done for you as an example.

Attorney: On the night of the murder, did you see my client enter room 167 of the Tropicana motel?

Witness: Yes, I did. I was sitting on a bench on the sidewalk when I saw a tall, thin man go into one of the rooms.

Attorney: **(1)** _Could it have been someone else_ ?

Witness: Oh, no; the person was definitely your client.

Attorney: **(2)** _____?

Witness: Definitely not; nobody else looks like your client. I recognized his mustache and hat.

Attorney: **(3)** _____?

Witness: It may have been; there are a lot of doors on that side of the building. But I went back the next day to check, after I read about the murder in the newspaper.

Attorney: **(4)** _____?

Witness: No, I don't think so. I clearly remember the location of the door; I just wasn't sure of the number on the door.

Attorney: Do you remember exactly what time it was?

Witness: Yes. The sun had gone down just a little while before I saw your client, so it was about 7:00.

Attorney: **(5)** _____?

Witness: I guess it could have been later, but not much later.

Attorney: Why were you sitting there, anyway?

Witness: I was just killing time.

Attorney: **(6)** _____?

Witness: Well, I had a little bit of wine with me, but it wasn't much.

Attorney: (7) _____?

Witness: That depends—how much is a lot?

Attorney: There was a nearly empty bottle of "Night Thunder" wine beside the bench you were sitting on.

Witness: Well, that's not a lot for me. I can drink much more than that.

Attorney: (8) _____?

Witness: Well, I've been in some treatment programs, but I wouldn't call myself an alcoholic.

Attorney: (9) _____?

Witness: Okay, so I may have been a little drunk. I still remember everything clearly.

Attorney: That will be all.

Exercise 6 *(Focus 6)*

Larry is angry at his son for how he dressed for a job interview. Suzanne is his wife; she feels that Larry is being too hard on the boy, and that a lot of the outcomes he predicts are not certain. Using the modals *would have, could have,* and *might have,* make Larry's predictions as certain as possible, and Suzanne's less certain and more polite. The first two have been done for you as examples.

Larry: I can't believe he didn't get a haircut before the interview! If he had gotten a nice crew cut like me, he **(1)** _____*would have*_____ gotten that job!

Suzanne: Now, dear, you never know. Crew cuts aren't as stylish these days; the boss **(2)** _____*might have*_____ felt the boy's hair was fine.

Larry: And his clothes—for crying out loud, what possessed him to wear those outlandish clothes to a job interview? If he had worn that suit I gave him he **(3)** _____ gotten more respect. I did when I wore it to my first interview.

Suzanne: If he had worn your ancient suit, the boss **(4)** _____ thought he stepped out of a time machine!

Larry: And he would have been impressed! My boss was.

Suzanne: You **(5)** _____ forgotten a few details, sweetie. I recall that it took you over a dozen interviews before you got your first job.

Larry: But the point is that I got it—just like our son **(6)** _____ if he had only dressed respectably.

Suzanne: Honey, the boss **(7)** _____ actually looked at our son's credentials instead of just his clothes. He has an excellent education, you know. And you shouldn't be so sure that he didn't get the job—he **(8)** _____. Didn't they say they would call him either way?

Larry: They **(9)** _____ called by now if he had gotten the job.

Suzanne: They **(10)** _____ had a hard time deciding—there were a lot of candidates for the job.

(*Telephone rings; Suzanne answers it and sounds excited.*)

Suzanne: You **(11)** _____ been a little more tolerant of your son. That was his new boss calling—he got the job!

Larry: Oh, really? Well, that's my boy! You know, dear, it is slightly possible that I **(12)** _____ been just a little bit wrong.

Exercise 7 (*Focus 7*)

Some of the perfective modals in the sentences that follow express contrary-to-fact meanings and some do not. Identify the modals that are contrary to fact. Then write down what meaning each contrary-to-fact modal has: (a) judgment of past event, (b) expectation or obligation, (c) result of a stated condition, or (d) result of an implied condition.

E X A M P L E : It's too bad that you failed your test, but you <u>should have</u> considered how much time you would have left to study after you got back from the beach last weekend. *a—judgment of past event*

1. You would have really enjoyed that course on the Ming dynasty; the instructor was great.
2. Weren't you to have graduated by now?
3. You could have graduated by now if you had taken courses last summer.
4. If you were having problems understanding the chapter, you should have called me.
5. The witness struggled to recall if the suspect could have been wearing glasses.
6. The game was supposed to have begun at noon.
7. Your parents could have stayed with us while they were here.
8. Jane could have at least called before she came over with her dogs.
9. Luis felt that he might have been overcharged.
10. If I had known that you wanted to go to the show, I would have bought you a ticket.

Exercise 8 *(Focus 8)*

Use the information in the first and second columns to express what will most likely have happened by the time period in the third column. You may want to add an **if** or **unless** clause to your sentence if you think it's needed.

E X A M P L E : June   The workers will be on strike   December
By December, the workers will have been on strike for 6 months.

8:00 A.M.	I will be working	8:00 P.M.
1895	The Johannsons own their farm	1995
January	Jason, at 260 pounds, promises to lose 10 pounds per month	June
present	The club shall elect its first president to a two-year term	two years from now
1996	Hong Kong becomes a part of China	2006
1998	Lisa begins work on her Bachelor's degree	2003

Stative Passives

Exercise 1 *(Focus 1)*

Underline all the passive verbs in the essay below. The first one has been done for you as an example.

In 1989, more motor vehicles <u>were produced</u> in Japan than any other country in the world. Although the United States is the world production leader for trucks and buses, 25 percent more passenger cars were manufactured in Japan than in the United States. More vehicles are bought by people in the United States than any other country on Earth, with 1 car per every 1.3 people. In Japan 1 car is found for every 4.3 people. In France the ratio is 1 to 2.5, and in Great Britain the ratio is 1 to 3.

Enormous profits are made in automotive manufacturing. In the United States, the first and second largest corporations are car companies (General Motors and Ford), and large portions of the economies of Japan, Germany, France, Italy, Canada, South Korea, and Brazil are devoted to automotive manufacturing. Cars are also manufactured in countries from Argentina to Sweden. In dollar amounts, more automobiles and automotive products are exported from the United States than any other commodity. Yet an even greater amount of automobiles and automotive products are imported to the United States.

More people are killed in auto accidents than any other type of accidental death. In fact, the rate is more than three times greater than falls, the second-leading cause of accidental death, and greater than the total deaths for falls, drowning, fires, accidental shootings, and poisonings combined. Auto accidents are listed as the eighth-leading cause of death in the United States. More lives are lost to auto accidents than to diabetes or AIDS.

There is some good news, though. Since 1970, the fatality rate for auto accidents in the United States has declined 30 precent. This decline was caused mainly by a number of improvements in the ways cars are designed. Nowadays cars in the United States are required to have either air bags or passive restraints, such as automatic seat belts. Energy-absorbing frames are found in most cars, along with reinforced-steel passenger compartments. Some more expensive cars are outfitted with antilock brakes, and most cars carry smaller safety additions such as eye-level rear brake lights and childproof door locks. Since 1970, tougher drunk driving laws have been passed in most states in the United States as well as mandatory seat belt laws in 36 states.

One issue that is related to car safety is thought to have had little effect. This is the general trend toward the manufacture of smaller cars. Over an 11-year period, the best-selling car models in the United States have changed from mostly full-sized cars in 1978 to mostly midsized and compact cars in 1989. This change is related both to rising gasoline prices and a decline in consumer confidence in larger American-made cars.

Exercise 2 (*Focus 2*)

Separate the passive verbs you underlined in Exercise 1 into stative and dynamic passives.

Stative passive	Dynamic passive

Exercise 3 (*Focus 3*)

Underline each *be* + passive form in the essay below and identify it as either a stative or an adjective participle. The first one has been done for you as an example.

Quick—where do you think the largest shopping mall in the world is? You might be surprised (*adjective participle*) that it isn't in Tokyo or Seoul or Los Angeles, and it is found in neither the United States nor Japan. You might be intrigued to know that it is located in what is described as "the coldest major city in the world," where temperatures in the winter routinely plunge to −40°F (−40°C). It is 12 hours by car from the nearest port, and closer to the Arctic Circle than to any of the world's hundred largest cities. Give up? It is called *The West Edmonton Mall*. Are you still confused? It is located in Edmonton, Canada, in Alberta province, the second westernmost of Canada's 10 provinces.

Are you surprised? Most people are; they wonder how something so big came to a town of only 600,000 residents. But how big is big? Well, the 5.2 million feet of space is filled with more than 600 stores and a few extras to ensure that shoppers are never bored. For example, when customers are tired of shopping, they can ride one of the mall's indoor roller coasters or try bungee jumping. If they aren't interested in these, there is a full-sized skating rink, an 18-hole miniature golf course, and three movie theaters with 19 screens. Oh, there's also an indoor lake with a life-size replica of one of Columbus' ships, and four submarines—more than the entire Canadian Navy.

Why Edmonton? Basically, the mall's owners said, "Why not Edmonton?" The four Iranian-Canadian Ghermezian brothers came to Edmonton in the 1970s with the money they had made selling carpets in Montreal. They opened the first third of the mall in 1981. It was designed to be large, but nothing near the largest. It was labeled that later on, after the second and third parts of the mall were built.

At first, the mall's size was considered the reason for its success; later, this formula was reversed. Now, more than 25 million visitors come to Edmonton to swim, skate, and above all, to shop. The mall's success has produced imitators, most notably the world's second largest mall, The Mall of America, in Bloomington, Minnesota—population 86,335.

Why Bloomington? Why not Bloomington!

Exercise 4 (Focus 4)

State the rhetorical function of stative passives in each of the following sentences, using categories from the charts given in your textbook on pp. 80 and 81.

E X A M P L E : The nation of Cape Verde is found in the Atlantic ocean off the west coast of Africa. *Describe location or position.*

1. Water is made of two parts hydrogen and one part oxygen.

    _____

2. In the British system, liquid measures below a pint are measured in gills.

    _____

3. The combination of one part oxygen and two parts deuterium oxiden is known as "heavy water."

    _____

4. Two-thirds of the earth is covered by water.

    _____

5. The molecules of water are connected to each other by a process termed "ionic bonding."

    _____

6. A peninsula is surrounded by water on three sides.

    _____

7. The sulfuric water which is found in geysers and hot springs is considered to be therapeutic.

    _____

8. Water turbines are used to produce electricity from dammed water.

    _____

9. Fish ladders are designed to allow salmon to swim over dams as they go upstream to spawn.

   _____

10. Lakes Huron, Ontario, Michigan, Erie, and Superior, which are collectively termed *The Great Lakes*, are found in the United States and Canada, and are known as the largest body of fresh water in the world.

    _____

Exercise 5 *(Focus 5)*

Each of the following sentences has one verb form error. Correct the errors.

E X A M P L E : Russians who opposed the communist revolution are sometimes call White Russians. *are sometimes call__ed__ White Russians*

1. Dumplings are steamed or boiled bread dough filling with fruit, meat, or vegetables.

   _____

2. Almost all Koreans are fond of kim chi, which is regard as their national food.

   _____

3. The V-shaped bone find in the upper breast area of poultry is believed to have special powers in some cultures.

   _____

4. Specially trained pigs are used to search for truffles, regarding as a kind of delicate gourmet fungus.

   _____

5. Zhong zi is a Chinese food made with rice, meat, and vegetables wrap in banana leaves.

   _____

6. Fortune cookies, although regard as a Chinese food, were invented in the United States and are never served in China.

   _____

7. Recipe ingredients in the United States are measure in cups and spoons.

   _____

8. Paella is a kind of seafood and vegetable stew serve on a bed of rice.

   _____

9. Cilantro is also know as Chinese parsley.

   _____

10. People around the world cook with garlic, an onionlike bulb that is actually relate to lilies.

    _____

Article Usage

Exercise 1 *(Focus 1)*

For each of the following pairs of sentences, circle the letter before the sentence that makes a general versus specific reference about the italicized noun or noun phrase. Note that different references are not always marked by different articles.

E X A M P L E : (a.) The *X-ray tube* was invented by Dr. Coolidge.

  b. Technicians replaced the *X-ray tube* on the old machine.

1. a. Years ago, *pharmacists* used to carry items such as garlic and leeches.

  b. The *pharmacist* filled a prescription for Suzette.

2. a. *Identical twins* share the same genes.

  b. The couple had *identical twins* last fall.

3. a. *Casts* are one of the oldest forms of medical treatment still in use.

  b. After Jennifer fell off the truck, the doctor put *casts* on both of her arms.

4. a. A technician used a *microscope* to examine the blood sample.

  b. The *microscope* was invented in 1590.

5. a. *MRI* (magnetic resonance imaging) is used to detect problems in soft tissues.

  b. Ngoc's *MRI* revealed a slightly torn ligament in her knee.

6. a. A *gerontologist* specializes in the diseases of the elderly.

  b. A *gerontologist* on TV said that people with weak bones should take calcium supplements.

7. a. *Radiologists* are trained in the use of X-rays.

  b. *Radiologists* at Central Hospital went on strike.

8. a. Marieta told a *nurse* that her mother had high blood pressure.

  b. A *nurse* needs at least two years of education and state certification.

9. a. The patient flinched when the doctor put the *stethoscope* on his chest.

  b. The modern *stethoscope* has been in use for over 150 years.

10. a. *Doctors* have complained about the rising costs of malpractice insurance.

 b. *Doctors* at Central Hospital have never had a malpractice suit brought against them.

Exercise 2 *(Focus 2)*

Some of the sentences below contain mistakes in usage of abstract generic *the*. Correct the mistakes.

E X A M P L E : The eraser is used to remove pencil marks. (*Eraser* is a simple inanimate object)

1. The cheese is made from milk.
2. The light bulb was invented by Thomas Edison.
3. The movable type was invented by Johannes Gutenberg.
4. The blue whale is the largest mammal in the world.
5. The left-handed people die on average earlier than others.
6. The diamond is the hardest stone.
7. The hydrogen is the first element on the atomic table.
8. The nectarine is a cross between the peach and the apricot.
9. The tie is worn by many executives throughout the world.
10. The Arabian horses are prized for the speed and beauty.

Exercise 3 *(Focus 3)*

Complete the sentences below with (*the*) + plural nouns.

1. Concerted efforts against ivory poachers have brought _____ back from the brink of extinction.
2. _____ are required to visit Mecca at least once during their lives.
3. _____ speak Tagalog.
4. Conservationists around the world are working to save _____, black and white spotted bears found only in parts of China.
5. _____ are proud of their country's pyramids, the Nile River, and the Suez Canal, among other things.
6. With auto companies such as BMW and Mercedes-Benz, _____ have proven themselves to be excellent automobile manufacturers.
7. _____, led by Mao Zedong, drove the Nationalists out of China in 1949.

8. _____ have suffered the loss of Mohatmes Gandhi, Indira Ghandi, and Rajiv Ghandi to assassins.

9. The guerilla commander led _____ to victory over the government.

10. _____ and the West Germans were reunited in 1990, when the two countries became one again.

Exercise 4 (Focus 4)

Some of the following sentences contain mistakes in usage of the article a(n) to describe a generalized instance of something. Correct the sentences that are wrong.

EXAMPLE: A tongue is the strongest muscle in the body. (*The tongue*)

1. A cheetah is the world's fastest land animal. _____

2. A seismologist studies the factors that produce earthquakes. _____

3. A photovoltaic cell is the heart of all modern electronics. _____

4. A compact disc was invented by RCA. _____

5. A sirocco is a hot wind that blows from the east. _____

6. A professor in a university is usually required to have a PhD. _____

7. A liver is responsible for cleaning blood. _____

8. A potato is native to the Americas. _____

9. A computer makes editing one's mistakes much easier. _____

10. A stomach digests food. _____

Exercise 5 (Focus 5)

Fill in the blanks with a word of your own choosing plus an article, where necessary.

EXAMPLE: *Soap* is combined with water to make an alkaline cleaning solution.

1. _____ is a black-and-white-striped, horselike animal found in Africa.

2. _____ are used by astronomers to study the stars.

3. _____ is used to pound in and remove nails.

4. _____ are used to fix teeth.

5. _____ is a sport played with nine players, a bat, and a ball.

6. _____ is an insect that begins life as a caterpillar before it acquires its beautiful wings.

7. _____ is frozen water.

8. _____ is a sweet, chewable substance made from chicle, and sold under names such as Chiclets, Doublemint, and Juicy Fruit.

9. _____ is used to sweep floors.

10. _____ are worn to improve defects in vision.

Exercise 6 (Focus 6)

Fill in the blanks with the names of the illnesses given below, plus the appropriate article where necessary, and the correct form of *be*. More than one answer may be correct in some instances.

EXAMPLE: *Arthritis is* (is/are) a disease that primarily affects the joints.

1. _____ (is/are) also known as "the black death"; spread by flea-infested rats, it killed millions in Europe during the Middle Ages.

2. _____ (is/are) spread primarily by animal bites.

3. _____ (is/are) a fever-producing disease common in tropical regions and spread by mosquitos.

4. _____ (is/are) a common winter illness that produces mild body aches and a runny nose.

5. _____ (is/are) the common name for an illness similar to the common cold but more severe and is caused by several types of virus.

6. _____ (is/are) an illness peculiar to deep-sea divers who rise to the surface of the ocean too quickly.

7. _____ (is/are) the formal name for the flu.

8. _____ (is/are) a fatal, incurable disease transmitted primarily through sexual contact and the use of contaminated IV needles.

9. _____ (is/are) a sudden occurrence of heart failure.

10. _____ (is/are) an open sore, often found in the stomach and produced by stress.

Exercise 7 (Focus 7)

Fill in the blanks with the correct body part and the correct form of the verb given. Pay special attention to article usage.

EXAMPLE: <u>The navel is</u> (is/are) the scar left on the stomach from the removal of the umbilical cord.

1. _____ (pump/pumps) blood throughout the body.
2. _____ (cover/covers) the outside of the body.
3. _____ (filter/filters) wastes from the bloodstream.
4. _____ (is/are) used to hear.
5. _____ (is/are) used to speak and eat.
6. _____ (is/are) skin covering the head.
7. _____ (is/are) enlarged through exercise.
8. _____ (enable/enables) humans to think.
9. _____ (is/are) used in breathing.
10. _____ (is/are) used to smell with.

Exercise 8 (Focus 8)

Find an article in an encyclopedia, textbook, or magazine such as *Scientific American* which deals with a technological advancement or invention. Some good topics might be the fax machine, the compact disc, the microprocessor, the photovoltaic cell, the cellular phone, or the personal computer. Examine all the abstract generic uses of *the* that you find. Do they occur often in the subject position of a sentence? Are they more prevalent in the introductory section of the text?

Exercise 9 (Focus 9)

Fill in the blank of the first sentence in each pair below with an unmodified noun. For the second sentence, use the same noun plus a modifier.

EXAMPLE: <u>Elephants</u> are the largest land mammals. <u>African elephants</u> are the larger of the two main elephant species.

1. _____ are the unhatched young of birds. _____ are most commonly eaten.

2. _____ are four-wheeled transportation machines. _____ are produced in Japan.

3. _____ are the opposite gender of men. _____ have husbands.

4. _____ are jewelry worn on the fingers. _____ signify marriage.

5. _____ are worn to protect the feet. _____ are used to run in.

6. _____ is the heaviest component of milk, and is often used in coffee. _____ is a creamy white dessert topping.

7. _____ are places where goods are sold. _____ are places where food is sold.

8. _____ is a beverage made from coffee beans. _____ has no cream or sugar in it.

9. _____ are round objects used in many different sports. _____ are used to bowl with.

10. _____ are competitions to see which contestant can move the fastest. _____ are competitions to see which horse can move the fastest.

UNIT

7

Reference

Exercise 1 *(Focus 1)*

Underline the reference forms (*it*, *they*, *the* demonstrative and *such* reference) that refer to information in previous sentences. Put brackets around the referents. There may be more than one reference form in a sentence.

E X A M P L E : ["What does she want?"] ["Why won't he listen?"] <u>Such questions</u> are probably familiar to all couples.

1. Tannen's book was a best-seller because she articulated communications difficulties that are common to many couples. Before her book, many of these were seen as personal failures rather than cultural differences.

2. At work and at home, miscommunication between the sexes is especially problematic. These areas have benefitted the most from Dr. Tannen's findings.

3. Couples who understand the implications of Dr. Tannen's research should have a better understanding of their own relationship. Such knowledge would surely improve a relationship.

4. Dr. Tannen was not the first person to notice gender-based language differences. As one example, these have been noted among the speech and writing of Japanese women for years.

5. Linguists have noted, for example, that many Japanese women tend to use intonation patterns that are never found among men. The patterns in general are of a sustained higher pitch.

6. Also, one of the Japanese alphabets known as *hiragana* was originally used primarily by women. The reasons for this are somewhat obscure.

7. In recent times, gender-based behavior differences have long been the subject of jokes. Such humor hasn't always been kind, but it has at least been observant.

8. One perpetual question that women have about men is why they tend to switch TV channels so frequently. That is a question which Dr. Tannen has no immediate answer for.

9. Men often complain that women don't express themselves directly enough. This concern is addressed by Dr. Tannen, who feels that indirectness for women is both culturally imbued and regarded as more polite.

46

10. She also adds that few societies regard directness in speech as a virtue. Those that do are in the minority.

Exercise 2 (Focus 2)

For each sentence pair, underline *the* and the demonstrative reference in the second sentence and put brackets around its referent in the first sentence. Then state what type of reference is being used in relation to the referent: repetition of the entire referent, partial repetition, a synonym, or a paraphrase.

E X A M P L E : Most languages show some [gender-based differences]. <u>These differences</u> may be in very different areas, though. *Partial repetition*

1. Sex-based differences are found not just in tone and voice characteristics, but in the way the language itself is written. In English, these differences are found in the names of occupations and roles. _____

2. A number of occupations and role names for men become derogatory in their feminine forms. This abasement has resulted in lessened or modified usage of the feminine forms of many word pairs such as major/majorette, star/starlet, master/mistress, governor/governess, and mister/mistress. _____

3. Men's names are frequently modified for women, but the reverse rarely happens. Men's names such as Robert, George, Louis, and Paul have feminine counterparts (Roberta, Georgette, Louise, Paulette), but there are no male names for Elizabeth, Laura, Jane, or Katherine. _____

4. Women's names are often given the suffix *-ie* or *-y*. This diminutive suffix is found far less frequently in male names: Judy, Kathy, Patty, Tracy, Terry, and Betty are frequently found adult women's names, but Billy, Jimmy, Robbie, and Johnny are more often associated with boys than men. _____

5. In Japan, women also are traditionally given names with the suffix *-ko*. This suffix is the written character for "child," and is found in the common names Masako, Takako, Hiroko, and Keiko. _____

6. Wives in English-speaking countries have traditionally adopted their husband's names, but never the opposite—Mrs. John Smith, but never Mr. Mary Smith. This practice is changing, however. _____

7. There are also a number of insulting terms for females which have no male equivalent. Words with a negative connotation, such as *divorcée*, are almost exclusively applied to women. _____

8. A more subtle problem concerns words which have no overt sexual specification, but become sexist in some contexts. Words signifying hair color, for example, are gender-neutral as adjectives ("My brother has blonde hair"), but tend to signify females when used as nouns ("A brunette moved in next door"). _____

9. Another problem is caused by the use of masculine pronouns for universal reference ("Each student needs to bring his own pencil"). This problem is caused by the lack of a gender-neutral third person singular pronoun in English. _____

10. Offices and institutions often try to avoid sexist language with guidelines for nonsexist usage. However, these rules multiply so quickly that people tend to resort to what they began with—their own best judgment. _____

Exercise 3 *(Focus 3)*

Decide whether *it, they, them,* or *the* + noun phrase is appropriate for each blank. If *the* + noun phrase should be used, choose a noun phrase that fits the context.

E X A M P L E :   Angel and Luis both finished the season with 20 goals apiece. *The players* tied for the league scoring championship.

1. Javier: I read that women tend to smile more when they speak.
   Beatrice: don't believe _____! I know plenty of women, such as my boss, who *never* smile.

2. Pat is working on a thesis dealing with the difficulties of non-native English speakers learning final -*s*. She should finish _____ by July.

3. The student attitude survey found that students in general were pleased with the college, but would like to have more classes scheduled on nights and weekends, extended library hours, and better food in the cafeteria. _____ will be discussed at the next meeting of the college council.

4. The Bulls and the Suns played a tremendous game. However, _____ prevailed in the final minutes and won by a point.

5. The silk melons need to be fertilized every week, while the snow peas only need regular watering. While I'm gone, then, be sure to add some fertilizer when you water_____.

6. Lacewings, praying mantises, and ladybugs are beneficial to gardeners. _____ are beneficial because they eat parasitic insects, and thus control crop damage without dangerous chemicals.

7. Kim wants an interesting job and a good income. _____ are his main reasons for going to college.

8. In their last game, the Yankees hit poorly, made a number of fielding errors, and gave up 15 hits. The next day the coaches worked on _____ by hitting ground balls to the infielders.

9. Larry: I heard that you're selling your car.

   Yovanka: _____ true—are you interested?

10. The doctors found that the mysterious illness was hereditary, passed on through the father, yet could be treated with changes in lifestyle and minor drug treatment. _____ were published in a medical journal.

Exercise 4 (Focus 4)

Put an appropriate demonstrative form in each blank: *this, that, these,* or *those.* If you think more than one might be appropriate, discuss in class the contexts (including speaker attitude) in which each might be used.

1. Imelda: After I finish work on (a)_____ project, I'll be free to help you.

   John: But you've been working on (b)_____ project for months! Aren't you ever going to finish?

2. I do not agree with _____ people who oppose the council's recommendations.

3. After leaving her country to live in Italy for one year, Nelly then moved to Germany, and then Canada before she settled here. _____ is why she entered college a few years later than she wanted to.

4. Who made _____ muddy tracks on my clean carpet?

5. I heard that Pham had spoken in favor of the nominee. _____ made everyone confident that she must be good.

6. The median age for first marriages in the United States has risen by 15 percent over the last 30 years. During that same period, the divorce rate has more than doubled. _____ statistics lead one to expect that the birthrate has also declined, and it has—down 30 percent in the same time.

7. John, I'm asking you to look carefully at my plan. _____ is the best hope we have for getting the company out of debt.

8. You should beware of _____ schemes where you are offered a free vacation if you will only come listen to a sales presentation for condominiums.

9. Chapter 1 gave an overview of the nervous system. It gave descriptions and diagrams of the neuron, the brain, and the spinal cord. It showed the main nerves of the body, and explained how sensory charges were translated from electrical impulses into sensations. _____ chapter also gave a basic description of the main areas of the brain.

10. If we make our airline reservations immediately, we can save 50 percent. _____ seems like a great deal.

Exercise 5 *(Focus 5)*

Decide whether or not to use a demonstrative adjective (*this, that, these,* or *those*) to complete each sentence below. To explain your choice, use some of the reasons below (paraphrase from Focus 5 in your text; refer to it for examples and information). More than one answer might be possible.

Speakers use *this, that, these,* and *those*

    a. To place greater emphasis on the referent

    b. To avoid needless repetition of the referent, especially if it is long

    c. To more clearly signal a clause or sentence referent

Speakers avoid using *this, that, these,* and *those*

    d. In second mentions

EXAMPLE: Leon: Have you heard that the writing lab is going to get new computers and the language lab has received a dozen new tape machines?

           Amy: Yes, Dr. Wells told me about *that*. (c; "that" is used to more clearly signal a clause or sentence referent)

1. Did you watch the game last night? I've seen a lot of championship games, and _____ was the best ever.

2. This tomato doesn't have much flavor. What do you think of _____?

3. In the summer semester, classes meet at much closer intervals, so there is much less time to complete assignments. _____ is why you should carefully consider the type of class you take in the summer.

4. We're planning to visit St. Paul's the same day we go to Covent Garden, but we're not sure if there will be time for _____.

5. The book I'm reading now is pretty boring, but you should read the one I read before _____.

6. Jim: Did you know that we always see the same side of the moon?

   Mary: Be serious! Everyone knows _____.

7. _____ is the best meal you've ever cooked!

8. This homework problem kept me up until two o'clock last night. Do you know how to solve _____?

9. Lia: Have you heard that the school is going to build a stadium and start up a football team?

   Antonio: No, I hadn't heard _____.

10. They're calling for hail over the weekend. _____ is going to damage the crops if they're not protected.

Exercise 6 (Focus 6)

Underline the *such* reference in the following groups of sentences or dialogues. Then put brackets around the referent.

EXAMPLE: [A number of birds that were brought to the United States for their beauty] later turned into pests. Two such birds are the starling and the mute swan.

1. The committee searched for a candidate with good credentials and a solid work history. However, no such person could be found.

2. The business world was stunned by the company's relocation overseas. It was clear that such a move had been undertaken only as a last resort.

3. Patient: Ever since this project came up, I can't sleep at night, I've lost my appetite, and I'm very grouchy.

   Doctor: Such symptoms are common to stressful situations.

4. The candidate loved to meet with people and talk for hours. She would often stay at rallies to discuss issues long after the news reporters went home. She answered her own phone, and spent at least an hour a day reading and responding to letters from worried voters. Such actions built her reputation as someone voters could trust.

5. James: Did you know that Rudy and Zelda are going to get married?

   Inez: Married? Just a month ago they swore they'd never date again. Who could imagine such a thing!

6. Before we accept this contract, we need to buy a stabilization processor and a multireel film washer. Such equipment will be necessary to turn out photos as quickly as the client wants.

7. Abdul works late every night and rarely takes a day off. Such dedication to his work has earned him promotions and bonuses, but has also caused some problems with his marriage.

8. I wish you would reconsider your plan. Such a plan will be very hard to implement.

9. Some countries have political boundaries that coincide with their cultural boundaries, so that most of their citizens speak the same language and share the same general beliefs. Japan and Korea are two such countries.

10. You have to learn to get along with people who are not like you. Such people are found everywhere.

Exercise 7 (Focus 6)

Fill in the blanks with an appropriate reference using *such*.

EXAMPLE: The doctor said that Lisa needed to eat more spinach, kale, broccoli, and green beans while she was pregnant. _Such vegetables_ are high in the kinds of vitamins that her baby needs.

1. Some things you should do before you go on a trip are stop delivery of your mail and newspapers, put some of your lights on timers to come on at night, and have someone cut your lawn when needed. _____ will keep your house from appearing empty, and can help discourage thieves.

2. The social services board planned, among other things, to open another shelter and expand its present job training services. _____ were intended to reduce the number of homeless people in the city.

3. The store was always filled with customers, but every day it seemed there were more unexpected bills coming in—a leaky roof that had to be fixed, an increase in their fire insurance, and a lawsuit from an angry customer. _____ eventually drove the company into bankruptcy.

4. Rubella, mumps, and polio affect many children in poor countries. Sadly, _____ are preventable only if enough money is available for vaccines.

5. In Coatesville the team's fans overturned cars in the streets. In Glendale, they ran onto the field and tore down the goal. _____ resulted in the team's suspension from the annual tournament.

Exercise 8 *(Focus 7)*

The sentences below contain errors in the use of *the*, *it/they*, demonstratives, and *such*. Correct the errors; more than one answer may be possible.

1. The speaker last night believed that violent scenes in movies and on TV had a damaging effect on children. He said that violent scenes in movies and on TV dulled children's sense of right and wrong.

2. Dino is the kind of person who is never satisfied with anything, so don't worry about what he said about your paper. This person will always have something unkind to say about anything you do.

3. Did you see this story in the newspaper this morning about the immigrants whose boat sank just as they got near the shore? This story says that most of them swam ashore, but not all of them made it.

4. I had hoped to do my paper on deforestation and its effect on global warming, but someone else had already chosen it.

5. The basketball team acquired veteran center Dominic Bedrosian. The coach hopes that such a player will help the team a lot.

6. Much classical music has its origins in folk music. One such music is Dvorak's *Slavonic Dances*.

7. Sarah: I think that the minimum voting age should be lowered to 16.
   Rachel: I disagree with this.

8. Bob: What are you all going to see tonight?
   Ruben: *Ghost.*
   Bob: But this movie came out years ago—why not see something new?

9. Jorge: I read that an advice columnist found that 98 percent of her male readers felt that women had too many rights now. And then on the way to work this morning, a radio talk show host reported that 87 percent of his listeners had the same opinion.

   Larry: Come on, Jorge. I heard the exact opposite at a rally I went to last week. It all depends on who you're asking. To be valid, opinion polls have to be random; otherwise these statistics are worthless.

10. Before you leave the building, turn off the lights and lower the thermostat. This needs to be done before you turn on the burglar alarm.

Choose the <u>one</u> word or phrase that best completes the sentence.

1. _____ well known for their excellent breakfasts.
   - (A) English are
   - (B) The English are
   - (C) An English is
   - (D) English is

2. _____ are responsible for a large amount of the pollution of urban areas.
   - (A) Automobiles
   - (B) An automobile
   - (C) The automobiles
   - (D) Automobile

3. Hayat has _____ and won't be in school today.
   - (A) flu
   - (B) cold
   - (C) the flu
   - (D) the cold

4. Knowledge, desire to achieve, and an eagerness to work with others are important qualities in a worker. In fact, _____ are more important to the hiring committee than where a person went to school or what grades he or she made.
   - (A) qualities
   - (B) the qualities
   - (C) such qualities
   - (D) this

5. Your paper is to have been completed by the end of the next week. _____
   - (A) It should have been graded already.
   - (B) It wasn't double-spaced.
   - (C) Jane would have gotten an A if she had spent more time on it.
   - (D) Late papers will be lowered one letter grade.

6. You said that you had been waiting here for over an hour, but that _____—this place has only been open for 30 minutes.
   - (A) couldn't have happened
   - (B) should have happened
   - (C) might have happened
   - (D) would have happened

7. Luisa's engagement ring _____ by the waiter on the top of the restaurant sink.
   - (A) is found
   - (B) was discovered
   - (C) were found
   - (D) are found

8. A: It's a waste of money to attend State College.
    B: _____ true!
    - (A) This isn't
    - (B) They aren't
    - (C) That isn't
    - (D) These aren't

9. This experiment has been done hundreds of times before. If you had followed the directions carefully, you _____ the proper result.
    - (A) should have gotten
    - (B) might have gotten
    - (C) could have gotten
    - (D) can get

10. Jane would have made a great basketball player. _____
    - (A) She's training for the next Olympics.
    - (B) However, she chose to be a swimmer instead.
    - (C) She played center on the team.
    - (D) She's retiring at the end of next year.

11. Cigarette smoke can damage _____.
    - (A) a lung
    - (B) lungs
    - (C) lung
    - (D) the lungs

12. Modern technology has affected our language. _____ can be seen in words like *hookup, interface,* and *fax.*
    - (A) That influence
    - (B) The influence
    - (C) Influence
    - (D) This influence

Identify the one underlined word or phrase that must be changed in order for the sentence to be grammatically correct.

13. Participating in <u>normally enjoyable sports</u> can have <u>dire consequences</u> when people fail
                   A   **B**
    to exercise caution and lose control. <u>Such two sports</u> are skiing and sailing; sheer neg-
                                                 C
    ligence is responsible for many accidents in <u>these</u> sports.
                                               D

14. I <u>would never have done</u> what Sally <u>did</u>; she went over to pet a wild fox that <u>was sleeping</u>
          A   **B**   **C**
    in the woods and it bit her. She <u>should have not done</u> that.
                                        D

15. In a typical system <u>used</u> in advanced surgery and component therapies these days, a
                          A
    centrifuge drive, which <u>separates</u> blood into its four components, <u>is connected</u> to various
                             B   **C**
    pumps to deliver blood into and out of the system <u>by qualified technicians.</u>
                                                        D

16. Dear Mr. President: I have heard or read of many cases of people having operations and receiving bills for one hundred thousand dollars or more. This situation is terrible.
                                                                                                          A
<u>This situation</u> is so pernicious that the people in question are often forced to sell their
B
homes. I know you are aware of <u>this</u>. I only pray you can do something about <u>it</u>.
                                C   **D**

17. Eighteenth-century <u>wig makers</u> were also barbers, which meant that in addition to
                       A
making <u>the wigs</u>, they often <u>cut hair</u>, shaved beards, let blood, and <u>pulled teeth</u>.
       B   **C**   **D**

18. If computers <u>had not been invented</u>, how <u>could we have come to understand</u> such
                 A   **B**
vastly complex interrelationships such as those presented by global weather patterns?
How <u>could anyone supposed to have analyzed</u> the immensely complex data concerning
    C
flow and turbulence and <u>discovered</u> the equations that described these processes?
                          D

19. <u>The Barbary ape</u> is <u>a small tailless macaque</u> of Algeria, Morocco, and Gibraltar. Leg-
    A   **B**
end has it that <u>the British</u> will lose the Rock of Gibraltar should its small colony of
                C
<u>the Barbary apes</u> depart.
D

20. If you're sure that <u>you've tried</u> every key three times and that none of them <u>works</u>, I
                        A   **B**
<u>would say</u> that Peter <u>should have given</u> us the wrong ones.
C   **D**

21. The eastern bobcat <u>is sometimes known</u> as "the bay lynx" <u>averages</u> 15 to 20 pounds,
                       A   **B**
although every year a few males in the 30- to 35-pound class <u>are taken</u> <u>by</u> hunters or
                                                             C   **D**
trappers.

22. Must the Indians of Central America <u>have been</u> in contact with Asians in ancient times?
        A   **B**
There is a striking body of evidence based on a comparison of artistic and architectural
forms which <u>suggests</u> that there <u>was</u> probably some kind of interchange.
            C   **D**

23. Some conservationists and tropical biologists are beginning to become concerned
about <u>the survival</u> of <u>the strangler fig</u> because its life cycle is fragile, and its fruit is
      A   **B**
a dietary staple of <u>the tropical mammals and birds</u>.
         C   **D**

24. <u>Provided that</u> work on the new wing <u>is completed</u> according to plan, we <u>estimate</u> that
    A   **B**   **C**
manufacturing output <u>would have doubled</u> by the end of the next fiscal year.
                      D

25. When I first heard that <u>skunks and raccoons</u> searching for grubs could completely de-
                            A
stroy a lawn, I couldn't believe <u>them</u>, but now that <u>the same thing</u> has happened to my
                                 B   **C**
lawn, I know not to raise such doubt about <u>what</u> at first I don't understand.
                                           D

Object Complements

Exercise 1 *(Focus 1)*

Identify and underline each of the object complements in the following passage. Put brackets around the noun or noun phrase each complement refers to. The first sentence has been done for you as an example.

(1)I suspect that [some of the predictions in *Megatrends 2000*] are <u>accurate</u>. **(2)**The prediction about "downsizing" is reasonable. **(3)**Modern telephones, computers, and other consumer electronic goods are now smaller, lighter, and faster. **(4)**Their belief in global environmental cooperation is also good. **(5)**One country's efforts at environmental protection will be without much success unless its neighbors also cooperate. **(6)**Their prediction about war becoming obsolete is not supported by recent events, however. **(7)**Wars resulting from ancient hostilities are evidence that hatred will never become obsolete.

Exercise 2 *(Focus 2)*

Using the fictitious data from the tables below, fill in the blanks with the appropriate noun complements.

1994 *Daily News* poll of high school students
  Biggest hero: Carl Sagan
  Most inspirational leader: Bill Clinton
  Favorite book: *Lord of the Flies* by William Golding
  Favorite actor: Tom Cruise
  Favorite actress: Winona Ryder

1994 *Daily News* poll of older Americans
  Recent President who helped this country the most:
    1. Roosevelt
    2. Kennedy
    3. Reagan

1994 *Central State University* poll of history students

    Best U.S. Presidents:

        1st—Abraham Lincoln (Vice President—Andrew Johnson)

        2nd—George Washington (Vice President—John Adams)

    Worst U.S. Presidents:

        1st—Richard Nixon (Vice President—Gerald Ford)

E X A M P L E : The students *called The Lord of the Flies their all-time favorite book.*

1. In 1994, most U.S. high school students _____ Carl Sagan their _____.

2. They also _____ Tom Cruise their _____, and Winona Ryder their favorite actress.

3. They _____ Bill Clinton _____.

4. Older Americans _____ Roosevelt _____, with Kennedy in second place.

5. Most history students surveyed _____ Abraham Lincoln _____.

6. They also _____ Richard Nixon _____.

7. George Washington _____ John Adams _____. Adams went on to become the second U.S. president.

8. Richard Nixon _____ Spiro Agnew his Vice President in 1968, but Agnew was forced to resign in 1973 for tax evasion.

9. Before Richard Nixon resigned from the presidency in 1974, he _____ Gerald Ford _____, thus making Ford the first U.S. President not voted on in a national election.

10. Ford was not a popular president, though, and, after only two years in office, in 1976, voters _____ Jimmy Carter _____.

Exercise 3 *(Focus 3)*

Using items from the table below, make five sentences with noun complements and active structures, and five sentences with noun complements and passive structures.

Group 1	Group 2	Group 3
a. Michael Jordan	a. his readers	a. health experts
b. Terminator II	b. Martin Luther King's birthday	b. President Bill Clinton
c. Al Gore	c. Arly	c. his godparents
d. Jorge's new son	d. Vice President	d. a scary writer
e. swimming	e. its supporters	e. sportswriters
f. Pablo Picasso	f. an excellent form of exercise	f. a great painter
g. art historians	g. products of high quality	g. 49 state legislatures
h. Most Valuable Player	h. a state holiday	h. Japanese cars
i. many consumers	i. a poll of 1,000 movie fans	i. horror author Stephen King
j. The Republican Party	j. Best Film	j. The Grand Old Party
k. Britons	k. elevators	k. lifts

E X A M P L E : *Michael Jordan was named Most Valuable Player by sportswriters.* (passive)
The sportswriters named Michael Jordan Most Valuable Player. (active)

1. _____

2. _____

3. _____

4. _____

5. _____

6. _____

7. _____

8. _____

9. _____

10. _____

Exercise 4 (Focus 4)

Fill in the blanks with *as, for,* or ∅:

1. The panel found the expert's suggestions _____ ridiculous.

2. The victim's testimony was accepted _____ true by the court.

3. The police mistook the man _____ his brother.

4. We recognized the car _____ Jane's.

5. The referee declared the exhausted fighter _____ the winner.

6. Bananas are regarded _____ tropical fruit.

7. I considered the property _____ a good investment.

8. Jamaica is described _____ a beautiful island.

9. The greenhouse effect is accepted _____ true by many scientists.

10. Many people regard watching TV _____ a waste of time.

Exercise 5 (Focus 5)

Determine whether the sentences below are complete or not. If they are incomplete, finish them with either a noun or an adjective complement. There are several answers possible for each.

EXAMPLE: The jury found the defendant, and then the judge sentenced him to 10 years in jail. (Incomplete: The jury found the defendant *guilty,* and then the judge sentenced him to 10 years in prison.)

1. The research group proved the theory, so no one used it again.

   _____

2. The children imagined a monster under their beds, so they were afraid to go to sleep.

   _____

3. Mary's rude comments made John.

   _____

4. The company president listened to the employee's suggestions and found them, so he implemented them immediately.

   _____

5. Hong considers herself a great cook, but her food tastes terrible.

   _____

6. The guests considered Trang's cooking and asked for more.

_____

7. His rude way of speaking makes Felipe, so no one will go out with him.

_____

8. Solomon loved the movie, but Ruth found it boring.

_____

9. The Senators thought the plan, so they voted for it.

_____

10. When Jane discovered her wedding ring, she searched the house frantically trying to remember where she last put it.

_____

Exercise 6 *(Focus 6)*

Using the map given below, answer questions about the Fontaines' vacation in Washington, D.C. Fill in the blanks with appropriate *object + prepositional complement* combinations. The first one has been done for you as an example.

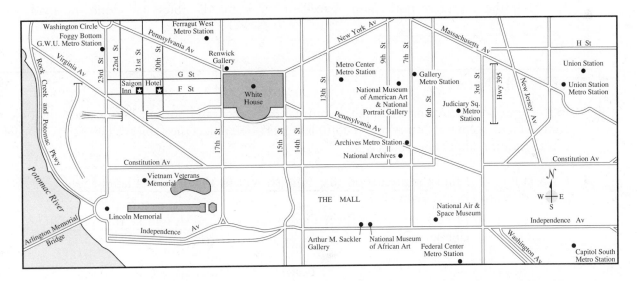

1. The Fontaines thought that their hotel would be miles away from the center of the city, so they were surprised when they arrived in Washington to find *their hotel in town*.

2. The next morning, they visited the Lincoln Memorial. Bill Fontaine, who fought in Vietnam, found _____, and so he walked over to see it.

3. They went to the White House, but the tours were already filled. However, Jane Fontaine, who teaches art in a high school, was delighted to discover _____.

4. From the Renwick Gallery they walked to the National Air and Space Museum. It was further away than they anticipated, but they finally found _____.

5. As they tiredly walked west along the mall looking for a Metro station to take them back to the hotel, Jane discovered _____, and so she quickly went in to look over its collection of Far Eastern and African art.

6. After they showered and rested a bit, they were glad to find _____. They went inside and had a great Vietnamese dinner.

Exercise 7 *(Focus 7)*   PAIR

Discuss with your partner ways to complete the following sentences with both noun complements and indirect objects. Discuss the differences in meaning.

1. After the Christmas rush, the toymakers decided to make Sue _____.

2. The talent scout found the young athlete _____.

3. After the executive noticed the excellent work his daughter had done, he made her

_____.

Exercise 8 *(Focus 8)*

In the sentences below, underline the grammatical object, and put brackets around the object complement. Remember that object complements often reflect the subject's perspective, belief, or observation about the object.

EXAMPLE : I find the prediction that English will be the universal language [questionable].

I find [questionable] the prediction that English will be the universal language.

1. The critics declared *Miss Saigon* the best musical drama since *Cats*.

2. The small company's managers considered worthless the suggestion that productivity and profits could be improved if only the company would spend several million dollars on robots.

3. The audience at the lecture found fascinating the speaker's presentation on the burial rites of Tibetans.

4. After an hour-long search, Sharon found in the far corner of her tattered sofa her car keys.

5. Everywhere he goes people mistake Ray for Elvis.

6. A recent survey shows that many people consider as true the idea that Elvis still walks the earth.

7. After deliberating for over an hour, the jury found the defendant guilty.

8. The panel found promising the planning commission's five-year plan for redesigning the downtown streets to accommodate more parking.

9. We took for granted Felicia's hard work until she took a job elsewhere.

10. The scientists proved false the projection of the ozone layer's total depletion within 20 years.

Relative Clauses Modifying Subjects

Exercise 1 (Focus 1)

Complete the adjective clauses of the sentences below using the information given about three small countries.

Liechtenstein
Population: 30,000
Government: Monarchy
Prime Minister: Hans Brunhart

Location: between Austria and Switzerland

Income: $22,300 per person
Capital: Vaduz—population 4,874
Brief history: The country was founded in 1719. It abolished its army in 1868, yet remained undamaged by any of Europe's wars since that time. The country is closely related to Switzerland, whose currency it uses. There is no unemployment, and taxes are low. Liechtenstein today has the distinction of being the world's largest exporter of false teeth.

Nauru
Population: 9,500
Government: Parliamentary
President: Bernard Dowiyogo (elected 1989)

Location: Pacific Ocean, 2,500 miles southwest of Hawaii

Income: $10,000 per person
Capital: Yaren—population 5,590
Brief history: The island was annexed to the German Empire in 1886. After World War I, the island was administered by Australia. During World War II, Japan occupied the island. In 1947, Nauru was put under the trust of the United Nations, and again administered by Australia. Finally, on January 31, 1968, Nauru became an independent state. There are no taxes on the island, and the literacy rate is 99%.

San Marino
Population: 20,000
Government: Republic
Co-regents: elected every 6 months

Location: Northern Italy

Income: $17,000 per person
Capital: San Marino—pop. 2,339
Brief history: According to tradition, San Marino has been in existence for over 16 centuries, making it the oldest state in Europe and the oldest republic in the world. Although it has a tradition of peaceful government and friendly relations, the country has been politically active, losing two soldiers in World War I, being occupied by the Nazis (and bombed by the Allies) during World War II, and today maintaining a standing army of 80 soldiers. Although the economy is diverse, its largest source of income is the sale of postage stamps to collectors.

EXAMPLE: The country *that has* the highest standard of living is *Liechtenstein*.

1. The country _____ the Pacific Ocean is

   _____.

2. The country _____ tradition names as the oldest country in Europe is _____.

3. Nauru is the only country _____. The other countries are governed by a Prime Minister and Co-regents.

4. The country _____ by Australia for over 50 years is

   _____.

5. The country _____ is the Swiss franc is

   _____.

6. The country _____ stamp collectors love to go to is

   _____.

7. The Prime Minister _____ Liechtenstein votes

   _____ in 1978 is _____.

8. The country _____ two soldiers in World War II is

   _____.

9. The country _____ an independent state in 1968 is

   _____.

10. The country _____ the Nazis

    _____ in World War II is _____.

Exercise 2 (Focus 2)

Following are nine items that many people consider necessary for a long and happy life. For each item, make a relative clause that specifies the qualities of these items.

EXAMPLE: a job

A job that pays a reasonable salary and is personally rewarding is necessary for a long and happy life.

1. a spouse

   _____

2. housing

   _____

3. children

_____

4. friends

_____

5. leisure time

_____

6. a hobby

_____

7. an education

_____

8. a boss

_____

9. a neighborhood

_____

Exercise 3 (Focus 3)

Where possible, reduce the relative clauses in the following sentences.

1. The manager whom we met was very polite.

2. The computer which is at the end of the row is out of order.

3. The crowd cheered the runner who was trying to regain the lead.

4. Students who are dedicated can be found in the library on Saturday nights.

5. Customers who do not have their receipts unfortunately cannot return their merchandise.

6. We were impressed with the paintings which we saw at the museum.

7. The president who was elected in November saw his popularity decline in March.

8. The parking place which is near the entrance is reserved for the Employee of the Month.

9. Workers who were angry confronted the union leader about the new contract.

10. Programmers who have experience with UNIX systems will be given first consideration.

Exercise 4 *(Focus 4)*

Rewrite the following dialogue in a less formal style by using less formal forms of the relative pronouns given. If this is not possible, mark the clause *NP*.

E X A M P L E : **Jeremy:** Ted will be one of the students with whom I will be studying.

Ted will be one of the students I will be studying with.

Elizabeth: Have you met the other students with whom you will be going to Ecuador?

Jeremy: Not yet, although the ones to whom I have spoken seem just as excited as me. We're all biology majors and are very excited about going to the Galapagos.

Elizabeth: Is that the first place to which you will go?

Jeremy: No; first we're going to spend some time in Quito observing some of the plants and animals of the Andes mountains. The people with whom we will be staying are also biology students, so I'm sure they will have a lot to teach us about the area. We'll spend the second week doing fieldwork in the Galapagos.

Elizabeth: That really sounds exciting. For what purpose is your research?

Jeremy: We want to compare some of Darwin's notes from his visit and our observations today, to see how things have changed—if in less than 150 years evolution has produced any results that we can measure.

Elizabeth: That really sounds exciting!

Exercise 1 (Focus 1)

In the following pairs of sentences, punctuate the sentence that contains the nonrestrictive relative clause. Then, explain why the information contained in the nonrestrictive clause is additional or incidental to the meaning of the sentence.

1. a. My boss who spends most of the time angry yelled at me again today.

    b. My boss who is always angry yelled while the other one quietly agreed.

2. a. Velcro which holds two pieces of material together with no moving parts was invented by a Swiss man in 1948.

    b. I was surprised when I learned that my cousin could not tie his new shoes because of the Velcro that held his old shoes together.

3. a. The McDonald's which is near the campus is a favorite place for students to meet.

    b. McDonald's which was founded by Ray Kroc is the largest restaurant chain in the world.

4. a. We were loudly discussing the election with Jenny who was sitting with us.

    b. We were loudly discussing the election with the woman who was sitting with us.

5. a. You need to drop this package off at the school which is on Route 7, just before you get to the bridge.

    b. You need to drop this package off at the school which is where the craft fair will be held this weekend.

6. a. Personal computers which have large hard drives and expanded memory are needed to run many new programs.

    b. Personal computers which are rapidly becoming less expensive and more powerful are frequently used in place of the old mainframe machines.

7. a. Many of the early European explorers and colonizers traveled in search of pepper which was used widely as a food preservative.

    b. Pepper which has been ground with the husks on is known as white pepper.

8. a. The goalie broke her nose which she had broken in the playoffs last year.

    b. The forward broke his finger which he had injured earlier.

9. a. Over the break Jose visited some friends in a city on the Pacific coast.

    b. Over the break Maria visited some friends in Campeche, which is on the Yucatan Peninsula of Mexico.

10. a. Our company has a picnic in the park which is where my husband proposed to me.

    b. Our company has a picnic in the park which the employees chose because it was the closest to most of their homes.

Exercise 2 *(Focus 2)*

Put brackets around all the nonrestrictive relative clauses and circle the head noun for each one. The first one has been done for you as an example.

(1) (Lonely Planet guidebooks), [which are put together by an Australian company,] have become indispensable guides for adventurous travelers around the world. (2) Tony and Maureen Wheeler, who are Lonely Planet's founders, started the series with an account of how they traveled overland from England to Australia in 1973. (3) Two years later they wrote *Southeast Asia on a Shoestring,* which continues to be one of Lonely Planet's consistent best-sellers. (4) Other adventurous travelers submitted ideas for similar books which covered places not on typical group tours. (5) Soon, books which dealt with countries in the Middle East, Africa, and South America were being produced, along with the original guides to Southeast Asian countries. (6) Now Lonely Planet, which has offices in Australia and the United States, offers more than 60 titles on places as diverse as Tibet, Yemen, and Micronesia.

(7) The guides, which are written by experienced teams of travelers and give credit to literally hundreds of other advisors, are all remarkable for their commonsense presentation of an astonishing breadth of highly useful information. (8) *China: A Travel Survival Kit,* for example, offers its reader information on everything that a traveler might need from hitchhiking to spitting to available blood reserves, in case of emergency. (9) Lonely Planet's philosophy, which states that "travelers can make a positive contribution to the countries they visit both by better appreciation of cultures and by the money they spend," has led the company to make contributions to a number of groups and organizations which are working to improve the countries written about in the series. (10) In 1987, $30,000 was donated to organizations like Greenpeace, which worked to stop French nuclear testing in the Pacific.

Exercise 3 *(Focus 3)*

Below are tools, instruments, and accessories from various fields. Where possible, identify the tool and identify a field it is typically used in.

E X A M P L E : A plumb bob, which is a pointed weight at the end of a string, is used for land surveying and bricklaying. Or: A plumb bob, whose string always points in a straight line, is used in land surveying or bricklaying.

1. microscope

_____

_____

2. T–square

_____

_____

3. bobbin

_____

_____

4. spatula

_____

_____

5. hoe

_____

_____

6. stethoscope

_____

_____

7. ledger

_____

_____

8. rolling pin

_____

_____

9. scalpel

_____

_____

10. trowel

_____

_____

11. handcuffs

_____

_____

12. periodic table

_____

_____

13. barometer

_____

_____

14. compass

_____

_____

15. lathe

_____

_____

Exercise 4 *(Focus 4)*

Below is an informal story that Lydia is telling about her recent trip. Fill in the blanks with restrictive relative clauses.

E X A M P L E : I made a photocopy of my passport before she left, *which was smart*.

(1) I also put all of my money into traveler's checks, _____.

(2) However, I forgot to make notes of which checks I had spent, _____,
because of what happened later. **(3)** I left my purse in the hotel room while I went downstairs for breakfast, _____.

   (4) When I got back to the room, I found the door open and my purse missing,
_____, so I called the manager. **(5)** She said someone had
stolen one of the master keys to the hotel, but she had not changed the locks yet,
_____. **(6)** When I asked her why she hadn't done this,
she said she had hoped it wouldn't be a problem, _____.

(7) The thief had stolen not just my purse with all my money and my passport, but also my camera, and the watch that my mother had given to me for my eighteenth birthday,

_____. **(8)** When I asked the manager if she would help

me replace any of the stolen items, she said that it wasn't her fault, _____

so much that I left without paying.

    (9) Outside the hotel, I called the number to report my stolen traveler's checks, and the

operator was very helpful, _____. **(10)** However, because

I couldn't tell her which checks had been stolen and which had been spent, I could only

cancel the checks I knew I hadn't spent, _____. **(11)** My

passport replacement was easier; I just went to the embassy with my photocopy, and they

gave me a new passport that afternoon, _____.

Exercise 5 *(Focus 5)*

Lydia is still talking about her trip. Fill in the relevant information using quantifiers in each
nonrestrictive noun clause given.

E X A M P L E : I really enjoyed meeting people in the countries that I visited, *most of whom*
               were very friendly.

(1) In Italy, I visited a number of art galleries, _____

contained Boticelli's *The Birth of Venus*. **(2)** After I had so many problems staying in

hotels, _____ I enjoyed, I decided to stay in hostels,

_____ were cheaper than even the lowest-priced hotels.

(3) The hostels in France were especially nice, _____

was a converted seventeenth-century monastery. **(4)** The other people in the hostels,

_____ were from Europe, Japan, or Australia, were

fun to be with and had a lot of good ideas about places I should see next. **(5)** I espe-

cially liked the Australians, _____ I traveled to England

with. **(6)** In London we visited the British Museum and the Victoria and Albert Museum,

_____ we loved. **(7)** We also traveled north to the Lake

District, where we hiked through several small towns, _____

was the home of the poet Wordsworth. **(8)** The Australians had relatives all over the

globe, _____ had an apartment in Edinburgh, so we

went north to stay with her for a night. **(9)** She introduced us to some of her friends,

_____ took us to a place that had all-night dancing.

Relative Adverbials

Exercise 1 *(Focus 1)*

Substitute relative adverbials for prepositions + *which* whenever possible. Make other necessary changes. Discuss why in some cases a relative adverb cannot replace a relative pronoun.

EXAMPLE: The Christmas season, during which some retailers do more than half of their annual business, is the busiest holiday in the United States

The Christmas season, when some retailers make more than half of their annual sales, is the busiest holiday for Americans.

1. The day on which Christmas is celebrated for Protestants and Roman Catholics was set by the Roman Church in 336.

_____

_____

2. One of the reasons for which December 25 was chosen was a preexisting festival in the now-dead Zoroastrian faith.

_____

_____

3. Early Christian leaders were worried about the way in which Zoroastrians practiced their religion because of its resemblance to Christian rites.

_____

_____

4. They hoped that the way in which they overlapped the holidays would enable followers to easily convert to Christianity.

_____

_____

5. Christmas only became popular in the middle ages, during which it became so popular that some Christians objected to some of its rituals.

   _____

   _____

   _____

6. Early Protestants in particular disliked the manner in which it was celebrated, leading to a ban on Christmas in England for part of the seventeenth century.

   _____

   _____

   _____

7. Santa Claus is the name which eighteenth-century New Yorkers gave to Saint Nicholas, a fourth-century bishop from Asia Minor (now Turkey).

   _____

   _____

   _____

8. The patron saint of children, Saint Nicholas was celebrated on a holiday apart from Christmas, on December 6, on which someone dressed as the bishop and distributed presents to small children.

   _____

   _____

   _____

9. There are many reasons for which the two holidays of Saint Nicholas' feast day and Christmas merged.

   _____

   _____

   _____

10. In general, both holidays have themes of gratitude and generosity, especially toward children, which might account for the way in which December 25 now is marked both by an infant (Christ) and a large man in a red suit who gives presents to children (Santa Claus).

    _____

    _____

    _____

Exercise 2 (Focus 2)

Part A. Match each of the time periods in the first column with an event in the second column. Then make sentences, using relative adverbials + an appropriate head noun.

EXAMPLE: July 4/Americans celebrate their independence
July 4 is *the date on which* Americans celebrate their independence.

1. Ramadan
2. Asian Lunar New Year
3. the nineteenth century
4. 1969
5. From noon to one o'clock
6. 1945
7. November 22, 1963
8. Winter
9. the Meiji Restoration
10. 11:59 on December 31, 1999

a. World War II ended
b. many workers stop for lunch
c. U.S. President John F. Kennedy was assassinated
d. most Asians cook delicious meals and give gifts of money
e. Queen Victoria ruled England
f. people go skiing
g. Neil Armstrong became the first person to walk on the moon
h. Muslims refrain from eating in the daytime
i. the first Japanese constitution was written
j. people will prepare to enter the third millennium

1. _____
2. _____
3. _____
4. _____
5. _____
6. _____
7. _____
8. _____
9. _____
10. _____

Part B. Now match places with events. Again, make sentences using an adverbial clause with an appropriate head noun. Try to use nouns other than *place* if possible.

EXAMPLE: Istanbul/Europe and Asia meet

Istanbul is *the city where* Europe and Asia meet.

1. downstairs
2. Mecca
3. north
4. the east coast
5. Saudi Arabia
6. the capitol
7. long-term memory
8. short-term memory
9. a cemetery
10. Argentina

a. the 1978 and 1986 World Cup champions are from here
b. most Americans live here
c. your name is stored here
d. every Muslim must make a pilgrimage here
e. a house is coolest here
f. a compass needle points here
g. a government meets in this building
h. about one-third of all the world's oil is located here
i. what you eat for breakfast is stored here
j. people are buried here

1. _____
2. _____
3. _____
4. _____
5. _____
6. _____
7. _____
8. _____
9. _____
10. _____

Part C. Now match reasons to statements. Give a statement for each match.

1. its friendly people
2. a chance for a better life
3. their better gas mileage
4. their aggressive offense
5. its strength and light weight
6. its irregular spelling
7. higher worker productivity
8. their size and aggressive behavior
9. decreased use of fluorocarbons
10. his sense of humor

a. the ozone layer is healing because of this
b. people immigrate for this
c. Brazil's soccer team is a two-time World Cup champion because of this
d. people buy compact cars for this
e. people like Charlie Chaplin for this
f. titanium is used in aircraft because of this
g. sharks have no natural predators because of this
h. businesses use machines for this
i. written English can be difficult because of this
j. tourists come to Egypt for this

1. _____
2. _____
3. _____
4. _____
5. _____
6. _____
7. _____
8. _____
9. _____
10. _____

Part D. Match the processes or methods in the first column to statements in the second. Make sentences for your matches, using the head noun *way* or adverb *how*.

1. inserting a toothpick to see if it comes out clean
2. weight training
3. letting cilantro go to seed
4. press conferences
5. an overtime period of 5 minutes
6. inattention to details
7. good customer service
8. being unafraid to make unpopular decisions
9. cutting back on the use of fossil fuels
10. studying hard

a. projects fail because of this
b. most top students make good grades
c. cooks check to see if baked goods are done by doing this
d. clients are kept by giving this
e. you get coriander in this manner
f. politicians disseminate information this way
g. the atmosphere will remain clean if we do this
h. basketball games tied at the end are decided this way
i. athletes build strength this way
j. politicians become leaders this way

1. _____
2. _____
3. _____
4. _____
5. _____
6. _____
7. _____
8. _____
9. _____
10. _____

Exercise 3 (Focus 3)

Match each of the places and times in the first column with events in the second column. Make sentences using relative clauses without head nouns.

EXAMPLE: Paris   the Eiffel Tower is located.
         Paris is *where* the Eiffel Tower is located.

78

1. 1990
2. Italy
3. 7–9 A.M. and 4–6 P.M.
4. Egypt
5. February
6. Central America
7. between January 21 and February 19
8. Orlando, Florida
9. evening
10. the Himalayas

a. Asian Lunar New Year falls
b. the world's tallest mountains are found here
c. the great pyramids are here
d. the Berlin Wall fell
e. St. Valentine's Day is celebrated
f. Walt Disney World is located here
g. Ferrari, Alfa-Romeo, and Lamborghini cars are made here
h. rush hour occurs in many large cities
i. when people eat dinner
j. Nicaragua and El Salvador are found here

1. _____
2. _____
3. _____
4. _____
5. _____
6. _____
7. _____
8. _____
9. _____
10. _____

Exercise 4 (Focus 4)

Rewrite 10 of the sentences used in Exercises 2 and 3 using the pattern *head noun + adverbial clause*. Add or delete words as necessary.

1. _____
2. _____
3. _____
4. _____
5. _____
6. _____

7. _____

8. _____

9. _____

10. _____

Exercise 5 *(Focus 5)*

Decide which form given (a or b) would be more typical or appropriate for the context, even though both may be grammatically correct. Below are some selected conditions from Focus 5; use them as a basis for the defense of your answers.

Head Noun Is Used

a. When the clause is the object of a preposition

b. To focus on or emphasize time, place, reason, or manner

c. When the meaning of the head noun is specific

d. When the context is more formal

e. When the head noun is the subject of a sentence rather than part of the predicate

Head Noun Is Not Used

f. When the meaning of the head noun phrase is general

g. When you can infer the head noun from context or from general knowledge

h. When the context is informal

1. Elizabeth: There's some mail for you.
   Mauricio: Oh great! Here is a letter from one of the schools _____.

   a. to which I applied   b. where I applied

2. I'm sorry to have to call you into my office, but I must tell you that _____ is unacceptable.

   a. the manner in which you   b. how you behaved
      have behaved

3. Bella: Do you remember when Ingrid is coming?
   Luigi: Let me think...Oh yes, she's coming _____ I'll be out of town.

   a. when   b. during the week in which

4. Do you know _____ the mail comes?

   a. the time in which   b. when

5. Did Jane say _____ she wasn't coming?

   a. why   b. the reason for which

6. Grethel showed me _____ I could buy stylish and inexpensive clothes.

      a. a second-hand store where   b. where

7. _____ students could study in groups would be nice.

      a. A place where   b. Where

8. The thieves drew a map of _____ they buried the money.

      a. where   b. the cemetery where

9. _____ did you want me to make your coffee, dear?

      a. In what manner   b. How

10. November is _____ Americans celebrate Thanksgiving.

      a. when   b. the month when

Exercise 6 (*Focus 6*)

Fill in the blanks with relative adverbials. The first one has been done for you as an example.

1. Chen looked back one more time at her home, *a place which* she was not sure if she would ever see again.

2. They began their trip in April, _____ the flowers were beginning to bloom and the world was beautiful.

3. We had a great vacation in the Caribbean, _____ the temperature was 20 degrees warmer than here.

4. 1968 was a watershed year in U.S. history, _____ both Martin Luther King and Robert Kennedy were assassinated, and U.S. troops sustained a major defeat in Vietnam.

5. Bhutan is a remote country in middle Asia, _____ until recent years has remained closed to most tourists.

6. Spring is a favorite time of year for many people, _____ the winter snows have gone and flowers begin to bloom.

7. I'll never forget my childhood, _____ I didn't have to worry about school or bills.

8. While we were in Taipei we visited the Palace Museum, _____ we saw, among other things, a cabbage that was made of jade.

Choose the <u>one</u> word or phrase that best completes the sentence.

1. The dog was found _____.
   - (A) with a blue collar around its neck
   - (B) it had a blue collar
   - (C) by the blue collar
   - (D) and the blue collar

2. Singapore, _____ is a city-state just south of Malaysia, has a total ban on chewing gum.
   - (A) that
   - (B) who
   - (C) which
   - (D) where

3. The coaches admired _____ the new player defended the goal.
   - (A) how
   - (B) the way how
   - (C) that
   - (D) in which

4. The student _____ won the contest received a $1,000 scholarship.
   - (A) whose essay
   - (B) who his essay
   - (C) which essay
   - (D) that his essay

5. The corporations _____ were interested in our project.
   - (A) which we spoke
   - (B) we spoke
   - (C) to which we spoke
   - (D) which to we spoke

6. Toronto is the city _____.
   - (A) which my sister moved
   - (B) my sister moved to
   - (C) my sister moved to it
   - (D) to that my sister moved

7. Edward has already taken algebra and chemistry. He found _____ difficult.
   - (A) it
   - (B) them
   - (C) these
   - (D) those

8. Lena regards her mother _____.
   - (A) for her greatest inspiration
   - (B) and her greatest inspiration
   - (C) as her greatest inspiration
   - (D) with her greatest inspiration

9. The period from the fourteenth to the seventeenth centuries, _____ the arts of ancient Greece were studied again in Europe, is known as the Renaissance.
   (A) was when
   (B) it was when
   (C) it was then
   (D) when

10. I brought home a wounded pigeon I found in the street, _____ was not a good idea.
    (A) that
    (B) who
    (C) which
    (D) where

11. The committee named _____.
    (A) Kim was president
    (B) Kim who was president
    (C) president Kim
    (D) Kim president

12. The joke _____ made Chris upset.
    (A) that I thought it was so funny
    (B) which I thought it was so funny
    (C) I thought it was so funny
    (D) I thought was so funny

13. A doctor _____ only on back pain is called a chiropractor.
    (A) whom works
    (B) which works
    (C) works
    (D) who works

Identify the <u>one</u> underlined word or phrase that must be changed in order for the sentence to be grammatically correct.

14. <u>The reason they hired</u> that construction firm to build the addition to their house
    A
    <u>was because</u> they admired <u>the way how they worked</u>, that is, their efficiency, their
    B   **C**
    speed, <u>and above all</u>, their attention to details.
            D

15. If you're intending to take courses <u>which</u> will lead to a science degree, <u>you probably</u>
                                          A   **B**
    shouldn't neglect to take a few liberal arts courses, <u>all which</u> will provide you with an
                                                            C
    important cultural background, <u>as well as</u> practice at expressing yourself clearly.
                                     D

16. Even though <u>the rewards are dubious</u> and <u>the risks quite high</u>, <u>places forbidden</u> will al-
                  A   **B**   **C**
    ways attract <u>daring and intrepid travelers</u>.
                   D

17. The club members <u>elected</u> Maria Ruiz <u>to be president</u>, <u>while</u> Carlos Guzman <u>was named</u>
                       A   **B**   **C**   **D**
    vice president.

18. They never explained the reason for why they were searching the train, but we had to
                            A
show our passports and then open our luggage, which they went through with embar-
                                              B
rassingly keen interest. It was the middle of the night when this occurred, and we had
                                                              C
to get off the train and wait on a platform that was dingy and cold for one hour before
                                              D
they allowed us to get back on.

19. Were you aware that the man with you spoke yesterday at the reception was a No-
                        A   **B**
bel prize winner whose research in medicine has led to a whole generation of cancer-
                  C   **D**
inhibiting drugs?

20. Taking advantage of the fact that masses of air often flow upward, creating a force
    A   **B**
called lift, large birds hitch a ride on a current of air and glide for hours without flap-
                                                          C
ping their wings. Lift, that acts as a kind of escalator to the clouds, comes in several
                  D
different forms.

21. When she was later asked about it, the former hostage said that the thing which for she
                        A   **B**   **C**
would always be grateful was her freedom.
          D

22. Joyce's mother made for her a new dress after the acting teacher had given Joyce the
                        A   **B**   **C**
leading role in the school play.
          D

23. When interviewed about their reactions to the new tax law, the majority of people
          A   **B**
called it outrageously.
    C   **D**

24. After Joan's first computer class, she remained at her desk and gazed with tired eyes at
                                      A
the long list of keyboard commands, of whose functions she could no longer remember,
                                      B
and she wondered if she would ever get the hang of such a complex machine.
                      C   **D**

25. The police mistook Arthur as another man who was wanted for the recent robbery of
              A   **B**   **C**   **D**
the Bay State Savings and Loan.

26. The place to where you go in London when you want a map of any place in the world
    A   **B**   **C**
is Stamford's. It's on Longacre, not far from Covent Garden, which is quite a tourist
                                                          D
mecca these days.

27. Galaxies whose low surface brightness due to fewer stars were, in the past, considered
            A   **B**
dwarfs. Recently astronomers have found that the actual mass of many of them is con-
                          C   **D**
siderably larger than suspected.

UNIT

12

Reference Adjectives and Adverbials

Exercise 1 *(Focus 1)*

Read the following pairs of sentences and discuss the differences in meaning of the identical adjectives.

1. (a) We need hard data for the story.
   (b) The data was hard to get.

2. (a) The President was late to the meeting.
   (b) The late President was fondly remembered.

3. (a) She is better now.
   (b) She is the better woman for the job.

4. (a) That's the exact paper I was looking for.
   (b) That paper is very exact; nothing is left to guesswork.

5. (a) That worker is simple.
   (b) That simple worker is humble in his ambitions.

Exercise 2 *(Focuses 2, 3, and 4)*

The first three types of reference adjectives you studied in this unit showed rank, lawful or customary relationships, and time relationships. Using the cues given, try to construct sentences using reference adjectives. (Of course, there are many possible answers.)

Reference adjectives showing rank: main, prime, principal, chief

Reference adjectives showing lawful or customary relationships: lawful, legal, rightful, true

Reference adjectives showing time relationships: original, previous, latter, former, present, future

EXAMPLE: Pyrite is a common metal with a false gold appearance.
True gold is rare.

1. The owner of the house right now doesn't take good care of it. I hope

   _____.

2. Two of the reasons Felipe came to this school are its pretty campus and good basketball team. However, _____.

3. Boxing champion Muhammad Ali acquired his name when he converted to Islam. _____ was Cassius Clay.

4. Ben Johnson won the Olympic 100-meter dash in 1988. However, he failed a postrace drug test, so Carl Lewis was named _____.

5. Before 1954, most blacks and whites in the United States attended separate schools. *Brown v. Board of Education,* argued before the Supreme Court that year, was _____ which changed that.

6. In 1979, the country we now know as Zimbabwe changed its name. _____ was Rhodesia.

7. The United States and the Soviet Union were the two world superpowers. However, only _____ still exists.

8. His supporters said that there were many reasons to vote for the president's plan, but _____ was that it would benefit the economy.

9. Jerry was given a ticket for going 15 miles per hour faster than the _____ speed limit.

10. The manager told the advertiser that his beautiful, artistic commercial failed to keep in mind the _____ purpose of advertising, which is to sell products.

Exercise 3 *(Focus 5)*

Decide how often each of the following events takes place. Then, make a sentence, using a reference adjective.

EXAMPLE: A full moon

A full moon is a monthly phenomenon.

1. Sunrise (phenomenon)

_____

2. Halloween (holiday)

_____

3. payday (occurrence)

_____

4. Big Ben's chimes (event)

_____

5. siesta (activity)

_____

6. The World Cup (tournament)

_____

7. robbery in New York City (occurrence)

_____

8. robbery in Tokyo (occurrence)

_____

9. flooding along the Nile (event)

_____

10. Tourism (industry)

_____

Exercise 4 *(Focus 6)*

See how many of the following geography questions you can answer.

1. In what part of Nepal is Mt. Everest?

_____

2. On what coast of Australia is Sydney?

_____

3. On what coast of Florida is Miami found?

_____

4. In what part of Turkey is Istanbul?

_____

5. In what regions of Africa do most people speak Arabic?

_____

6. In what part of the Arabian peninsula is Kuwait found?

_____

7. To what areas of most countries do people go when they want jobs?

_____

8. In what area of China do people speak Cantonese?

_____

9. Which part of Cyprus is mostly Greek? Which part is mostly Turkish?

_____

10. Which part of the island once called Hispaniola is now called the Dominican Republic? Which part is now called Haiti?

_____

Exercise 5 (Focus 7)

Some reference adjectives show the uniqueness of the noun. Answer the questions below using the reference adjectives *only, sole, single,* and *solitary* and an appropriate noun.

1. What is needed to start a fire?

   _____

2. What is needed to win a game?

   _____

3. What did the Soviet spacecraft *Vostok 1* carry?

   _____

4. What's the best one-hole score in golf?

   _____

5. Who was responsible for the invention of the light bulb, the phonograph, microphone, motion pictures, and 1,300 other inventions?

   _____

6. An old rhyme goes,

   For want of a nail the shoe was lost
   For want of a shoe the horse was lost
   For want of a horse the battle was lost
   For want of a battle the war was lost
   And all for the want of a nail.

   What lost the war?

   _____

7. Engagement rings in the United States typically display what?

   _____

8. What do we call a child with no brothers and sisters?

   _____

Exercise 6 (Focus 8)

Try to answer the questions below based on your knowledge of laws and customs common to North America. Use adjectives from Focus 8 in your answers.

1. A man married a woman in New York. Then, without getting divorced, he married another woman in California. Why was his second marriage illegal?

   _____

2. A student read an interesting article. Then she copied it and turned it in to her English teacher. Why was she expelled from school?

   _____

3. A salesman sold a piece of land to one person. Then he sold it to another person. Why was he prosecuted?

_____

4. A woman was found "not guilty" of a crime. Then the police found further evidence that she had, in fact, committed the crime, but they did not arrest her. Why not?

_____

5. Two scientists claimed that they had made an astonishing discovery. Other scientists criticized them when they were unable to duplicate the experiment. Why?

_____

6. A suspect was put in a lineup with other people, and two witnesses were separately asked to identify the criminal they saw. After the second witness made his choice, police had to release the suspect. Why?

_____

Exercise 7 *(Focus 9)*

Below are some selected statistics on careers. In the statements that follow, fill in the blanks using *adjective + noun*. The first one has been done for you as an example.

Occupation	Estimated Growth, 1990–2005
Electrical engineers	176,000
Occupational therapists	20,000
Preschool workers	490,000
Radiologic technologists	103,000
Registered nurses	767,000
Retail sales workers	1,381,000
Surgical technologists	21,000

1. More *radiologic technologists* will be needed as the population grows older and greater emphasis is placed on early diagnosis.

2. More _____ will be needed as more two-worker families look for child care situations that are more than babysitting.

3. More _____ will be needed due to the overall growth of the medical field.

4. More _____ will be needed as technological advances permit a larger number of outpatient surgeries, especially in clinics.

5. More _____ will be needed due to projected growth in retail sales.

6. More _____ will be needed as better medical procedures and safer automobiles enable more people to survive accidents, as well as the growth of the population in their forties, an age when the risk of heart disease and stroke increases.

7. More _____ will be needed as greater technological advances are made in the use of computers.

Exercise 8 (Focus 10 and 11)

Complete the dialogue below using the following words:

sheer   total   only   just   full   merely   utter

Inez: How was your trip?

Martin: It was the worst trip I ever had; a (1) _____ shambles from the first day.

Inez: Oh no! What happened?

Martin: Well, to start with, the airline lost my (2) _____ piece of luggage and it took a (3) _____ week for them to find it.

Inez: That's too bad. Did things go better after you got your luggage?

Martin: Not really. We were supposed to meet another tour group of students from the university at a temple outside of town, but the company had scheduled our trips at different times, so we met a group of (4) _____ strangers instead. By (5) _____ coincidence, however, I had met one person in the group several years ago in Kyoto.

Inez: That sounds nice—did you two do anything together?

Martin: Actually we did. She was interested in visiting the gardens on the south side of the city, so the next day we went there together. She taught me so much about horticulture! She said that she was (6) _____ a hobbyist, but to me she was an (7) _____ expert.

Inez: Well, it sounds like she prevented your vacation from being an (8) _____ disaster.

Martin: I guess so; with her, it was (9) _____ a fiasco.

90

Correlative Conjunctions, *Respectively*

Exercise 1 *(Focus 1)*

You are an advisor at New World Alternative College. Following is a partial list of offered courses for the fall on the college's two campuses. Advise students of course offerings, using correlative conjunctions where possible.

English Composition	M	19:30–22:00	Philadelphia Campus
	TTh	9:30–11:00	Wilmington Campus
Technical Writing	MWF	13:00–14:00	Wilmington Campus
	TTh	19:00–20:30	Wilmington Campus
Linguistics	W	17:00–19:30	Wilmington Campus
	TTh	8:00–9:30	Philadelphia Campus
Philosophy	T	17:00–19:30	Wilmington Campus
	M	17:00–19:30	Philadelphia Campus
Economics	MWF	13:00–14:30	Philadelphia Campus
Anthropology	T	19:30–22:00	Wilmington Campus
Astronomy	Th	19:30–22:00	Wilmington Campus
	F	11:00–1:30	Wilmington Campus
Physics	W	19:30–22:00	Wilmington Campus

E X A M P L E : **Tom:** I need to take English Composition and a social science course, but I can't drive to Wilmington.

Advisor: *You can take both English Composition and Economics at the Philadelphia Campus.*

1. **Lucy:** Can I complete my humanities requirements at the Wilmington Campus?

   Advisor: _____

2. **Tarek:** What can I take this fall to fulfill my social science requirement?

   Advisor: _____

3. **Leonore:** I can only come on Tuesdays and Thursdays during the daytime—is there anything I can take this fall?

   Advisor: _____

4. **Ricardo:** I'm registered for Philosophy right now—is that the only course you offer on Tuesday nights?

   Advisor: _____

5. **Abdul:** I'm registered for Expository Writing on Monday nights, but my boss might move me to the night shift next week—do you offer the course at any other times?

   Advisor: _____

6. **Tran:** When can I take Astronomy?

   Advisor: _____

7. **Li Hong:** Where can I take Linguistics?

   Advisor: _____

8. **Youn Sung:** I need to take a science course, but I work from one to nine P.M.—do you have anything I can take?

   Advisor: _____

9. **Larry:** Can I take a humanities course at the Philadelphia campus?

   Advisor: _____

10. **Moses:** I need a physical science course, but I work during the day—do you have anything for me?

   Advisor: _____

Exercise 2 (Focus 2)

Read each sentence. Write OK after sentences that are well-formed, parallel, and not repetitious. Rephrase the rest in concise, formal style.

EXAMPLE: Jorge won not only the game but also he won the record for consecutive championships. (noun phrase/sentence)

Jorge won not only the game but also the record for consecutive championships.
(noun phrase/noun phrase)

1. Since I left my country, I have become more responsible and a more independent person.

   _____

2. In the fall, not only will I take accounting, but also biology.

   _____

3. I both have been working very hard at my job and have been working very hard at school.

   _____

4. You either can come with us now or you can come with Lisa later.

_____

5. Not only did Imelda get into the honors program, but also Nelson.

_____

6. The board of directors decided both to open a Miami branch and to close the branches in Austin and Madison.

_____

7. People from both the Middle East and Latin Americans attended the conference.

_____

8. Marcus told me that either he would take his children to the museum or take them camping this weekend.

_____

9. You will need to either present a driver's license or major credit card to write a check in that store.

_____

10. I know neither where Alma is nor what she is doing.

_____

Exercise 3 (Focus 3)

As the manager of data operations for a small company, you need to hire someone to join your team of hardware and software experts. Evaluate the excellent qualifications of the applicants below. Respond to the questions using correlative conjunctions for emphasis.

Tony Perez	Emma Singh	Laura Park
B.S. in electrical engineering	B.S. in computer information systems	B.S. in electrical engineering
Experience with DOS and UNIX systems	Experience with DOS and UNIX systems	Experience with DOS
Three years experience as a programmer	Six years experience as a programmer	Eight years experience as a programmer
Trained in microcomputer repair	Not trained in microcomputer repair	Trained in microcomputer repair
Proficient in PASCAL	Proficient in PASCAL	Proficient in FORTRAN
Advanced knowledge of circuit design	Proficient in C	M.B.A.

(Continued)

Can start immediately	Can start by the first of the month	Can start at the end of the year
Applied to this company before	First time applicant	First time applicant
Extensive experience in mainframe software and design	Most experience limited to microcomputers	Most experience limited to microcomputers

E X A M P L E : Do any of the applicants have engineering backgrounds?

Yes, both Tony Perez and Laura Park have B.S. degrees in electrical engineering.

1. Do either of those two candidates also have advanced degrees in engineering?

   _____

2. Can any of the applicants work in UNIX?

   _____

3. If I wanted someone who knew how to fix computers as well as use them, who could I hire?

   _____

4. Do any of the applicants have more than 5 years experience in programming?

   _____

5. What kind of education does Laura Park have?

   _____

6. Do any of the applicants know PASCAL?

   _____

7. What computer languages does Emma Singh know?

   _____

8. We need someone soon—can any of them start before the first?

   _____

9. Do Laura Park or Emma Singh have experience with mainframe computers?

   _____

10. Other than Tony, have any of these applicants applied here before?

   _____

Exercise 4 (Focus 4)

Combine the following two sentences with *respectively*.

E X A M P L E : Spanish is the official language of Colombia. Portuguese is the official language of Brazil.

Spanish and Portuguese are the official languages of Colombia and Brazil, respectively.

1. Bahrain has a population of 500,000. Brunei has a population of 300,000.

   _____

2. Uruguay won the World Cup in 1970. Brazil won the World Cup in 1990.

   _____

3. The postal abbreviation for Michigan is MI. The postal abbreviation for Mississippi is MS.

   _____

4. The Blue Jays won by 2 runs. The Orioles won by 8 runs.

   _____

5. Volvos are made in Sweden. Renaults are made in France.

   _____

6. The average annual income in Chad is $158. The average annual income in South Africa is $1,890.

   _____

7. Niamy is the capital of Niger. Lagos is the capital of Nigeria.

   _____

8. Cantonese is spoken in southern China. Mandarin is spoken in northern China.

   _____

9. The compact disc was invented in the United States. The audiocassette was invented in Holland.

   _____

10. In Britain a truck is known as a lorry. In Australia it is called a ute.

   _____

Logical Connectors

Exercise 1 (Focus 1)

For each of the sentence pairs below, write down what the relationship of the second sentence is to the first: an added idea, an example, a similarity, a contrast, or a result.

1. One of the most fascinating and compelling myths of the ancient Greeks was that of Persephone and Hades. This story accounts for the seasons, the annual cycle of death and rebirth. _____

2. Hades was the god of the Underworld, of darkness and stillness. His brother, Zeus, was the god of the sky and the lord of storms. _____

3. Persephone was the daughter of Demeter, the goddess of fertility and agriculture. Like her mother, Persephone was associated with the ripening crops. _____

4. Hades was known as the "generous one" because he refused no one his hospitality, but he was also greedy and possessive. When he saw Persephone for the first time, he wanted her for himself. _____

5. Because of Demeter's pleading with Zeus, Hades was not allowed to keep Persephone in his realm perpetually. He had to allow her to return to the surface of the earth for half of each year. _____

6. Persephone rises in the Spring and remains with her mother throughout the long, warm days of summer. In the Fall, as the days get shorter and colder, she descends to Hades.

_____

Exercise 2 (Focus 2)

Provide the correct punctuation of the connectors in the following sentences if needed.

E X A M P L E : Herakles was much admired by the gods however he was despised by Hera.
Herakles was much admired by the gods; however, he was despised by Hera.

1. Ancient Egyptians saw the earth as an egg guarded at night by the moon, a great white bird. Similarly the early Christian Gnostics saw Heaven and Earth as a World Egg around which coiled a giant serpent.

_____

_____

_____

2. The study of geography owes a lot to Ptolemy who lived just less than two thousand years ago. The grid system which he adopted and improved remains in fact the basis of modern cartography.

_____

_____

3. Ptolemy drew upon the works of Strabo, another ancient geographer. Strabo was also an historian and one of the great travelers of his day.

_____

_____

4. Ptolemy's influence was considerable however he made some significant miscalculations.

_____

_____

5. Ptolemy prepared Europe for world exploring though having rejected the notion of the earth as a disk surrounded by the river Oceanus.

_____

_____

_____

Exercise 3 (Focus 3)

Use an appropriate sentence connector from the list below to signal the addition or alternative relationship expressed in the last sentence of each pair or group of sentences. More than one connector could be appropriate for most contexts. Try to use a different connector in each sentence.

also	what is more	in fact	on the other hand
in addition	as well	actually	as a matter of fact
furthermore	moreover	besides	alternatively

E X A M P L E : California is particularly prone to earthquakes. I experienced one just last week while I was there on a short trip.

__In fact,__ I experienced one just last week while I was there on a short trip. (other possible connectors: all intensifying additive connectors)

1. Fiona loves learning alphabets and can read and write Cyrillic. She has a grasp of Arabic, Hiragana, and Runes.

   _____

2. After Helen's operation, the doctor prescribed a potent antibiotic. She was given a painkiller.

   _____

3. I don't know how I'm going to manage to stay in shape this week with my crazy schedule. I've got a luncheon and dinner date every day of the week. I've even invited some people for tea tomorrow.

   _____

4. Nature is Patti's chief focus in life. When she's not working designing nature programs for children, she's out walking or sitting somewhere with binoculars or a magnifying glass.

   _____

5. Medical science has overcome many formerly fatal diseases. Smallpox has been eradicated. The incidence of tuberculosis and pneumonia has been greatly reduced or controlled.

   _____

6. All of knowledge owes a debt to the past. If we accept the current state of knowledge as final, we will never progress.

   _____

7. The object of the game is to capture all of your opponent's pieces. You have to avoid capture by your opponent.

   _____

8. We could listen to classical music. We could listen to rock.

   _____

9. It was so clear last night we could see thousands of stars. I could see all the individual stars of the Pleiades constellation. There were nebulae visible and galaxies.

   _____

10. I'm afraid I can't go out tonight because I'm broke. I can't even pay the electric bill this month.

    _____

11. In a recent survey it was found that more than half of the patients sought alternative treatments such as chiropractic, massage, vitamins, and herbs. Some tried acupuncture, biofeedback, and meditation.

    _____

Exercise 4 (*Focus 4*)

Use an exemplification, identification, or clarification connector from the list below that would be appropriate for each blank.

for example	to illustrate	that is	namely
for instance	in particular	in other words	specifically

1. Commerce has never been shy to borrow and profit from classical myths.

   (a) _____, we have Mercury automobiles, Midas mufflers, Ajax detergent, Zephyr and Bellerophon books, and Electra records to name but a few. Mobil gas stations, (b) _____, fly the banner of the winged horse, Pegasus.

2. The critics found the book tedious, egregious, and tendentious; _____, they detested it.

3. Medicine has borrowed heavily from Greek and Latin. Psychology, _____, with names such as the Oedipus complex to describe primal internal drives, owes a major debt to the ancients.

4. There is one thing you can do before you leave; _____, you can make sure that all the documents we worked on today have been backed up.

5. Greek and Roman place-names crop up everywhere in the eastern United States. Just glance at a map of New York State, _____. There we find the towns of Troy, Ithaca, Rome, Carthage, and Corinth among others.

6. You should never make anyone lose face; _____, you shouldn't do or say anything that will embarrass them in front of anyone else.

7. I don't understand the part about business expenses on the new tax form.

   _____, how does line *h* on page 2 relate to line *q* on page 4?

Exercise 5 (*Focus 5*)

Column A below has a list of general statements about spiders. Column B presents examples for each statement. Some examples, indicated in parentheses as "typical," are representative. Others, indicated in parentheses as "special," express the most important member. Make a sentence for each of the examples in Column B, using an appropriate connector.

E X A M P L E : When people see spiders, some feel disgust, *for example,* while some try to kill them, and some scream and run away.

Column A	Column B
1. Spiders are a very misunderstood group of arthropods	When people see spiders, some feel disgust, while some try to kill them, and some scream and run away (typical)
2. Spiders rarely do anything to harm us	Out of thousands of different spiders in the world, only a handful are poisonous to people (typical)
3. Some spiders bite people	Bites from black widows and brown recluses account for fewer fatalities than bites from bees and wasps (special)
4. Most spiders are actually very helpful	The most important predators of insects in the world, spiders protect plants by eliminating many harmful insects (typical)
5. Spiders display a great variety of habits and techniques in hunting	Orb spiders spin beautiful webs while wolf spiders and tarantulas stalk prey on the ground and ogre-faced spiders throw nets over their victims (typical)
6. Though most spiders live less than a full year, some are exceptions	Tarantulas do not become mature adults until they are 10, and females may live another 10 years after that (special)

1. _____
_____

2. _____
_____

3. _____
_____

4. _____
_____

5. _____
_____

6. _____
_____

Exercise 6 *(Focus 6)*

Some of the sentences below use **i.e.** or **e.g.** correctly; some do not. Identify which ones are incorrect and explain why.

EXAMPLE: The musical group Hesperus often offers programs of Americana, e.g., American folk and regional tunes played on historic instruments.

Incorrect—the second clause presents a clarification

1. The default font in the computer is Times; i.e., when you switch on the computer, the font that is automatically available for your work is Times.

   _____

   _____

2. Paul McCartney plays several instruments; i.e., not only does he play the guitar and piano but the trumpet and cello as well.

   _____

   _____

3. Many religions have dietary restrictions; i.e., Islam and Judaism both forbid the consumption of pork.

   _____

   _____

4. I've just finished an interesting article about Navajo cryptographers; e.g., the American Indians who coded and decoded messages during World War II.

   _____

   _____

5. American and British English can sometimes be quite different; i.e., in automotive terms, gas is petrol, a hood is a bonnet, and a trunk is a boot.

   _____

   _____

6. Certain fish are androgynous; i.e., they have characteristics of both sexes.

   _____

   _____

7. For insulation in cold, damp weather, high-loft synthetic fills are probably your best bet; e.g., Polarguard and Quallofil have proven reliability.

   _____

   _____

Exercise 7 (Focus 7)

In the sentence pairs below, the second sentence is repetitious. Rephrase or condense the information in these sentences and add a similarity sentence connector.

1. Among some of the people of the Pacific, there is an attitude that a person belongs to a specific piece of land even if he or she leaves home for a long period. Among the Greeks, there is an attitude that a person belongs to a specific piece of land even if he or she leaves home for a long period.

   _____

   _____

2. To become a hero, Theseus conquered the minotaur. Perseus conquered Medusa to become a hero.

   _____

   _____

3. In the Middle East it is taboo to eat with your left hand. In India it is taboo to eat with your left hand.

   _____

   _____

4. T cells help to maintain a healthy body by destroying abnormal cells before they proliferate. B cells help to maintain a healthy body by manufacturing antibodies.

   _____

   _____

5. Bonaventure Island off the tip of Quebec's Gaspé Peninsula is the site of a spectacular seabird colony during the summer. The Klamath Basin in California is the site of a spectacular waterfowl concentration during the autumn.

   _____

   _____

Exercise 8 (Focus 7)

The following chart gives information about some commonly used herbs. Imagine that you are a student investigating medicinal herbs, and that you have been asked to write a summary of the ways in which these herbs are similar. As preparation for your summary, use the information in the chart to make at least five pairs of sentences expressing similarity. Use a similarity connector with the second sentence of each pair.

EXAMPLE: Ginger promotes circulation; cayenne likewise aids this important bodily function.

Name of herb	Ginger	Dandelion	Chamomile	Echinachea	Cayenne
Part used	Root	Root or leaf	Flower	Root	Fruit
Systems affected	Stomach, intestines, circulation	Liver, kidneys, gallbladder, pancreas	Nerves, stomach, kidneys, liver	Blood, lymph	Stomach, heart, circulation, blood, respiratory
Properties/ actions	Stimulant, antigas, induces sweating	Diuretic, laxative, tonic	Nervine, tonic, induces sweating, sedative, antigas	Blood purifier, antimicrobial, antiseptic	Stimulant, antigas, antispasmodic, antiseptic, tonic, blood purifier
Indications	Promotes circulation, relieves fever, supports digestion	Stimulates kidneys; reduces inflammation; relieves congestion of liver, gallbladder, rheumatic pain	General calming action for restlessness, nervous stomach, and insomnia; relieves inflammation in mouth, throat, and eyes; supports digestion	Helps rid body of infections, restores proper bodily functions, increases health and vitality	Promotes circulation, supports digestion, relieves colds, headaches, and rheumatic pain, strengthens heart, relieves throat ailments
Preparation and dosage	Pour a cup of boiling water onto 1 teaspoon of fresh root and let infuse for 5 minutes; drink whenever needed	Put 2–3 teaspoons of root into one cup of water, bring to a boil, and simmer 10–15 minutes; drink 3 times daily Leaves may be eaten raw in salad	Pour a cup of boiling water onto 2 teaspoons of flowers and let infuse 5–10 minutes For throat, decoct half a cup of flowers in 2 liters water; allow to cool	Put 1–2 teaspoons of root in 1 cup of water, bring to a boil slowly, simmer for 10–15 minutes; drink 3 times daily	Pour a cup of boiling water onto $\frac{1}{2}$–1 teaspoon and let infuse 10 minutes; a tablespoon of the infusion should be mixed with hot water and drunk whenever needed.

(Information from David Hoffman, *The Holistic Herbal*, Findhorn, Moray, Scotland, The Findhorn Press, 1985; and Michael Tierra, *The Way of Herbs*, New York, Washington Square Press, 1983.)

Exercise 9 *(Focus 8)*

Use the information in the chart from Exercise 8 to make up five sentence pairs expressing differences between the herbs, their uses, and preparation.

E X A M P L E : Cayenne is a stimulant. Chamomile, on the other hand, is a sedative.

Exercise 10 *(Focus 8)*

Some sentence connectors may signal more than one meaning relationship. These include **on the other hand** (alternative, contrast, concession), **in fact** (intensifying addition, contrast), and **however** (contrast, concession). Write down which relationship each signals in the sentences below.

1. Judy got an A in English, French, and History. She didn't do so well, however, in Chemistry. _____

2. I think that Pedro is probably at home right now. On the other hand, he might still be at work. _____

3. The new Jeep is touted as being environmentally-friendly because its air-conditioning system does not use CFCs. On the other hand, it doesn't get very good gas mileage. _____

4. She thought everybody would laugh at her new hairstyle. In fact, hardly anyone noticed. _____

5. Parsley is a very flavorful and useful kitchen herb. In fact, it's excellent for the digestion. _____

Exercise 11 *(Focus 8)*

The chart below gives information about achievements that involved overcoming certain difficulties. Use the information to make up sentence pairs linked by a concession connector. Use a variety of connectors. The choice of subject nouns or pronouns is up to you as well as any other information you wish to add.

Difficulty	Achievement
1. Blizzards, extreme cold, avalanches	Reached the top of Mount Everest
2. Lost parents at an early age	Became renowned diplomat
3. Addicted to alcohol and drugs	Kicked the habits and became a better stockbroker
4. Settling into a new community	New friends and sense of inner strength
5. Car breakdowns	Got across the country

The expedition encountered blizzards, extreme cold, and avalanches. Nevertheless, they reached the top of Mount Everest.

1. _____

_____

2. _____

_____

3. _____

_____

4. _____

_____

5. _____

_____

Exercise 12 *(Focus 9)*

The two charts below give information about various characters from history, myths, and legends. Use the information from Chart A to make sentence pairs expressing reason–result relationships. Use Chart B to make sentence pairs expressing purpose relationships. For all sentence pairs, use an appropriate sentence connector.

E X A M P L E : Ariadne, the daughter of King Minos of Crete, gave Theseus a ball of thread. As a result, he was able to find his way out of the labyrinth after slaying the Minotaur.

Chart A

Character(s)	Event/Situation	Result
1. Ariadne, daughter of King Minos of Crete	Gave Theseus a ball of thread	Found his way out of the labyrinth after slaying the Minotaur
2. King Henry VIII of England	Wanted a male heir	Divorced his first wife
3. Adam and Eve	Ate the forbidden fruit	Were cast out of the garden of Eden
4. Tristan and Iseult	Drank the love potion intended for King Mark and Iseult	They fell deeply and tragically in love
5. Inanna, Sumerian sky goddess	Descended into the underworld and underwent death	Brought her beloved husband back to life

1. _____

2. _____

3. _____

4. _____

5. _____

Chart B

Character(s)	Action/Event	Purpose
1. The Aztecs	Sacrificed prisoners of war	Keep the sun in motion and increase the bounty of nature
2. Ulysses	Had his men plug their ears and had himself roped securely to the mast of his ship	Hear the song of the sirens and survive
3. James Bond	Risked his life	Save the world from megalomaniacs
4. Johnny Appleseed	Sowed seeds wherever he went	Spread apple trees around the United States

1. _____

2. _____

3. _____

4. _____

5. _____

TOEFL® Test Preparation
Exercises · Units 12–14

Choose the <u>one</u> word or phrase that best completes the sentence.

1. Lisa studied hard for _____ she made a good grade.
    - (A) her exam, yet
    - (B) her exam; consequently,
    - (C) her exam. Still,
    - (D) her exam, for

2. The star player broke his leg, _____ he won't play in the game next week.
    - (A) yet
    - (B) still
    - (C) so
    - (D) but

3. Students at State College can choose from a wide variety of majors; _____, there are degree programs in nursing, computer science, humanities, and agriculture.
    - (A) moreover
    - (B) besides that
    - (C) for example
    - (D) similarly

4. Fred bought the car stripped; _____, he bought it with no additional frills such as a radio or air conditioner.
    - (A) furthermore
    - (B) for example
    - (C) in other words
    - (D) especially

5. Naguib and Ahmed are a doctor and an architect, respectively. _____
    - (A) They can help you design your house.
    - (B) Naguib can help you design your house.
    - (C) Ahmed can help you design your house.
    - (D) It is impressive that each man could have two degrees.

6. Not only _____, she also set a new record.
    - (A) Sabrina won the race
    - (B) Sabrina did win the race
    - (C) did Sabrina win the race
    - (D) Sabrina wins the race

7. Leonard just got accepted _____.
    - (A) in a school that is medical
    - (B) in a school where is medical
    - (C) in a medical school
    - (D) in a school which is medical

8. I don't know that person you were talking to—she was a _____.
    - (A) stranger that was total
    - (B) total stranger
    - (C) very stranger
    - (D) very strange

9. A: Do you want to watch this program?
B: No; I saw the _____ last week.

(A) equal program

(C) same program

(B) program which was
the same

(D) program which was similar

10. The court ordered that the _____ of the property was the old man who paid $100 for it 50 years ago.

(A) law owner

(C) owner that was legal

(B) legal owner

(D) owner who was legal

11. _____ of the fire was a young boy.

(A) Only the survivor

(C) The only survivor

(B) The survivor that was
only

(D) The survivor only

12. We _____ Rome nor Florence; instead, we spent most of our time in Venice.

(A) didn't see neither

(C) saw neither

(B) did see neither

(D) neither saw

Identify the one underlined word or phrase that must be changed in order for the sentence to be grammatically correct.

13. The 1980s were a spectacular decade for Wayne Gretzky, the star hockey player with the Edmonton Oilers. From 1981 to 1987 consecutively, he was the NHL's leading scorer
  <u>A</u>
and winner of the Ross trophy. And every year from 1980 to 1987, however, he was
  <u>B</u>   <u>C</u>
the NHL's MVP and winner of the Hart Memorial trophy. In addition to these trophies
  <u>D</u>
and distinctions, Gretzky won several other awards and became a highly paid celebrity.

14. Natalie didn't think she would have enough energy to go to the concert tonight.
Not only she had stayed up half the night working on her thesis, but she also did some
  <u>A</u>   <u>B</u>
volunteer work in the morning and jogged in the afternoon. She is both tired and de-
  <u>C</u>   <u>D</u>
serving of rest.

15. J. Robert Oppenheimer was a brilliant physicist who was nuclear. Though he was
  <u>A</u>
in charge of America's first atomic bomb project, he utterly disapproved of the con-
  <u>B</u>   <u>C</u>
struction of hydrogen bombs in the 1950s.
  <u>D</u>

16. We often have a hard time in our family deciding where to go together for vacation. Last summer, <u>for example</u>, my mother wanted to go to the Aegean. My father,
    A
<u>on another hand</u>, insisted that he needed a dose of cold weather. The high Himalayas
    B
or the Andes <u>were his alternatives</u>. My sister wanted to visit Japan, and I had my heart
    C
set on the Australian outback. <u>As a result</u>, we all went our separate ways.
    D

17. <u>Both</u> Peter Paul Rubens and Anthony Trollope were men of many talents; Rubens was
    A
<u>both</u> a painter and a diplomat, <u>respectively</u>, while Trollope was a doctor <u>as well as a</u>
    B   **C**   **D**
novelist.

18. Non-native plant species have taken a major hold on this country. <u>In fact</u>, in the last
                                                                        A
10 years more habitat has probably been lost to exotic plants than to development.
<u>Alien plants</u> (i.e., Scotch and French broom, pampas grass, ice plant, and eucalyp-
    B
tus) are prolific in California. <u>Likewise</u>, kudzu is so widespread in the southern states
                                  C
that <u>it is known as</u> the vine that ate the south.
    D

19. The goal of all this research is <u>principal</u> to discover a <u>fast-reacting</u> process we can
                                      A   **B**
easily <u>replicate</u> and <u>which</u> will yield consistent results.
       C   **D**

20. <u>In the wake of</u> a break-in last year <u>in which they lost</u> $50,000 worth of crystals and
    A   **B**
gems, Mr. and Mrs. Caruso installed a hi-tech security system in their home and around
their property. <u>Moreover</u>, they bought a German shepherd dog. <u>Despite of these precau-</u>
                 C   **D**
tions, someone still managed to get into their house and make off with a priceless Van
Gogh.

21. A: Do <u>either</u> of you have to take French or Spanish this semester?
           A
    B: I'm <u>taking neither</u>. I've finished my language requirement.
             B
    C: I'm not sure yet. I think I'll take <u>both</u> Russian or Chinese.
                                            C
    A: Good luck. <u>Those languages are not only</u> complex, but they have different alpha-
                   D
       bets too.

22. <u>Many of the latest studies</u> concur that <u>a sole parent</u> has a much more challenging
    A   **B**
time raising a child and making <u>the monthly payments</u> than do married couples,
                                 C
even <u>those on limited incomes</u>.
     D

Discourse Organizers

Exercise 1 *(Focus 1)*

Make up a sentence with a beginning sequential connector that could follow each of the sentences below. Try to use a variety of connectors.

E X A M P L E : Money is always a problem. *To start with*, I never seem to have enough of it.

1. Money is always a problem.

_____

2. Building a house involves many different activities.

_____

3. When I was a child I had several chores to do.

_____

4. To make a pot of tea, follow these steps.

_____

5. I can make some recommendations about how to learn a language.

_____

6. Bringing up a child is no simple task.

_____

7. Today, stress is a fact of life.

_____

Exercise 2 *(Focus 1)*

For the sentences below, write a list of ideas that could follow, using beginning, continuation, and concluding sequential connectors in your list. Try to use a variety of connectors.

E X A M P L E : If I won the lottery and become a millionaire, I would be overjoyed. *First of all, I'd throw a big party. Next, I'd find a beautiful place to live. Finally, I'd take a long vacation and travel around the world.*

1. If I won the lottery and become a millionaire, I would be overjoyed.

_____

_____

2. Writing a research paper is hard work.

_____

_____

3. Summer is a great time.

_____

_____

4. Staying in good shape takes commitment.

_____

_____

5. To keep my car running smoothly I do some important things.

_____

_____

6. Reading is one of the best ways of improving your language.

_____

_____

7. Sleep is wonderful.

_____

_____

8. A good husband (or wife) has the following characteristics.

_____

_____

Exercise 3 *(Focus 2)*

E X A M P L E : Fill in the blanks with appropriate words or phrases studied in Focus 2. Use different forms of connectors for each passage. Add commas where needed.

1. _____ two basic _____ of spiders. _____ are web builders. _____ are wandering spiders.

2. _____ three major _____ of rocks, classified into groups determined by how they were formed. _____ is igneous rock which crystallizes from molten magma or lava. _____ is sedimentary rock which forms in layers or strata and often have fossils. And _____ is metamorphic rock which has been changed considerably from its original igneous, sedimentary, or metamorphic structure and composition.

3. _____ several significant _____ in which Marx went beyond the philosophy of history of his day. _____ the activity of human working populations was more important to him than philosophical abstractions. _____ he replaced a closed system of speculation with a critical philosophy which attempted to unify theory and practice. _____ he asked revolutionary questions, such as what constitutes the alienation of labor. _____ he turned his history of human labor into a criticism of labor in society.

4. _____ a few _____ regarding the extinction of the dinosaurs. _____, and perhaps the most popular, is that the earth was hit by a meteor, and the dust from the impact blocked out the light necessary to maintain adequate plant life. _____ theory holds that rather than something coming from outer space, there was a gigantic volcanic explosion that threw huge quantities of dust into the atmosphere. _____, _____ the more farfetched explanations such as the expansion of the swift and stealthy mammal population which had developed a great appetite for dinosaur eggs.

5. _____ four remarkable _____ about the universe that encourage us to investigate whether we are alone. _____ is that space is transparent. A ray of starlight can speed unhindered through space for hundreds of millions of years. _____, the universe is uniform. Wherever we look, everything appears to be built out of the same chemical elements we find on Earth. _____, the universe is isotropic; that is, it looks essentially the same in every direction. Every observer sees galaxies stretching off into all parts of the heavens, just as we do. _____, the universe is abundant. Within the range of our telescopes lie perhaps one hundred billion galaxies, each home to around one hundred billion stars. From such perceptions has arisen the enterprise called SETI—the search for extraterrestrial intelligence in the universe.

Exercise 4 *(Focus 3)*

Write a summary statement for each of the sentences or brief passages below. Use the summary connector indicated in parentheses. For statements that will introduce topics, make up any sentence that fits the context.

EXAMPLE: This report will examine the impact of the arms industry on the increasing violence in the world. (briefly)

Summary statement: *Briefly, there is a strong link between the arms industry and the rising tide of violence in the world.*

1. My presentation will focus on the effects on the globe of greenhouse gases. (briefly)

   _____

   _____

2. Ladies and Gentlemen of the jury. We have heard here today the testimony of expert witnesses. It is now well established that my client was miles from the scene of the crime when the events in question took place. And what is more, the weapon found in the glove compartment of my client's car could not have fired the bullet found lodged in the door at 76 Ocean Boulevard. (in short)

   _____

   _____

3. The consensus has too often been that the 1950s were a dull decade characterized by bland mediocrity and timid conformity. Recent books, however, have begun to alter our perceptions of this misunderstood and curiously maligned period. When we look closely at the canvases of Pollock and de Kooning, when we listen carefully to the music of Miles Davis, the poetry of the Beats, and the voices of the burgeoning movements for social justice, we recognize passion and creativity, not caution. (all in all)

   _____

   _____

4. So far, I have examined some prevalent ideas about lung cancer. (as has been previously mentioned)

   _____

   _____

5. Biological diversity is the key to mankind's survival. Only by conserving the vast variety of plant and animal life, using and sharing it wisely, can we hope to feed everyone adequately and meet the challenges of a rapidly changing world. (in summary)

   _____

   _____

6. Our company has never had a better year. Our stock has made gains consistently through-out every quarter. We've more than doubled our profits over those of last year. We've added five hundred new employees to our payroll, and on the drawing board are plans for a new production plant. (overall)

_____

_____

7. These are a few health tips to take into consideration when visiting Nepal. Watching what you eat or drink while in Kathmandu and on the trail is critical. Tap water and river water are strictly off limits unless boiled briskly for at least 20 minutes. Some people have successfully used water filters. Raw fruits and vegetables should be avoided unless they've been completely peeled. (in summary)

_____

_____

8. The lifesaving benefits of automotive air bag systems are well-known. What isn't well-known is that many components, including the bag itself, are all made of plastic. Plastic makes a lot of things safe. For example, plastic packaging keeps medical equipment sterile and harmful medicines out of the hands of children. Plastic wraps and trays keep food fresh and safe. And shatter-resistant plastic bottles have prevented thousands of accidents. (briefly)

_____

_____

Exercise 5 (Focus 4)

Write a question that might be used to begin a written essay or a speech for at least eight of the following topics. Ask a classmate to tell you which one he or she finds the most intriguing.

E X A M P L E : Peace: _Can peace be achieved without justice first?_

Injustice	Disease	Household responsibilities
The depletion of the ozone layer	Building a space station	Winter
The arms industry	Segregation	Evolution
World War II	Insects	National Parks

Exercise 6 (Focus 5)

The excerpts below are from the beginning paragraphs of books, articles, or essays. For each, predict what the rest of the text might be about.

1. Why should there be such an extraordinary variety of animals all doing the same things? Why should a whale have warm blood and lungs, whereas a similarly-sized swimming monster, the whale shark, has cold blood and gills? Why do indigenous Australian mammals rear their young in a pouch whereas mammals in the northern hemisphere retain their offspring within a womb and nourish them by means of a placenta? (From *The Trials of Life* by David Attenborough. Boston: Little, Brown, 1990.)

2. Does it take you more than ten minutes to unearth a particular letter, bill, report or other paper from your files (or piles of paper on your desk)? Are there papers on your desk, other than reference materials, that you haven't looked through for a week or more? Do magazines and newspapers pile up unread? Do you frequently procrastinate so long on a work assignment that it becomes an emergency or panic situation? (From *Getting Organized* by Stephanie Winston. New York: Warner Books, 1978.)

3. How many times have you thought about giving money to a cause, but you can't find one that addresses more than one issue? Is there a way to ensure that your donations affect both cultural and environmental preservation? (From "Cottonwood Foundation" by Genevieve Austin. *Buzzworm,* May–June 1993.)

4. Thinking about buying a computer that the whole family can use? How will it serve everyone using it? Is it for entertainment, education, tracking family finances, running a small business, or all of the above? (From "The Whole Family Computer Guide" by Christine Begole. *Home,* September 1993.)

5. Do we want to wait five minutes or more every time we have to cross the street? Does every green space have to be filled with a house or a shop? Do we all have to breathe fumes? When is enough enough? (From a letter to the editor in the *Brattleboro Reformer.*)

Exercise 7 (Focus 5)

Write a leading question to express each of the following opinions. More than one form is possible, and some ideas may need to be rephrased, not just transformed into a question. State the positive implication of each in parentheses.

E X A M P L E :   Opinion: Tropical rain forests are important for the whole planet. Possible questions and implications:

Aren't tropical rain forests important for the whole planet? (They are.)

Doesn't the whole planet benefit from tropical rain forests? (It does.)

Shouldn't we preserve tropical rain forests? (We should.)

1. All young children need to be vaccinated.

   _____

   _____

2. The sales of handguns should be regulated.

   _____

   _____

3. We waste too much money on the administrative side of our health care system.

   _____

   _____

4. Winter is a great time for a vacation.

   _____

   _____

5. It's better to be safe than sorry.

   _____

   _____

Exercise 8 *(Focus 5)*

State the negative implications of the following rhetorical questions taken from various published texts.

1. Should your children have to struggle with the same difficult and confusing dictionary you did?
   (Thesis: There is an excellent new dictionary available for your children.)

2. That high-priced box of sugar-coated cereal may taste good, but two slices of bread and a glass of milk is equal to the entire box in food value. How many slices are in a loaf? Even with the more expensive whole wheat breads, I can buy two loaves for the cost of one box of cereal. Who needs all that sugar anyway?
   (Thesis: Consumers need to be aware that junk food is more expensive than foods with high nutritional value and has potentially bad side effects.)

3. Reginald Denny's rescuers, unknown to each other but impelled by similar purpose, came from different places and just clambered onto his truck or into the truck, or led the way for the truck to escape [from his attackers]. There's not a single one of the old standbys that they couldn't have invoked: What could they do, being just an individual or two against a mob? Wouldn't this just be a feel-good venture that would leave the basic problem unaffected, the problem of the stresses between the races and the classes of the community? And, in any case, weren't they doomed to fail? There are always powerful reasons to just stay at home and profess your virtue and fantasize your valor and maybe even blather about the need for caring and sharing and the rest.

   (Thesis: There are heroes in our society who are willing to risk their lives for human and moral reasons.)

4. Stereo A has all the buttons and switches and flashing lights you could ever desire, but is it the gadgets that deliver the sound that you want? Stereo B has none of the gizmos above. Its simple case and elegant finish house superb and durable circuitry. And what's more it costs less.

   (Thesis: In choosing a sound system it's quality, not elaborate features, that counts.)

5. The generals announced their long-awaited truce with an aerial bombardment (fireworks, their press called it). Freedom of speech meant shutting up anyone who had anything to say. This is liberty? This is peace?

   (Thesis: the military powers were following a policy of deception and hypocrisy.)

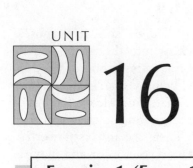

16

Conditionals

Exercise 1 *(Focus 1)*

Decide whether *if, only if, even if,* or *unless* should be used in each blank.

The Struggle for Equality

A major theme throughout history is the struggle of particular groups against prejudice and segregation. Just thirty years ago, in many parts of the American South, **(1)** _____ you were white you couldn't sit at the front of a bus nor eat at certain restaurants. Furthermore, blacks were barred entry to many universities and colleges in the South **(2)** _____ they had excellent high school grades. **(3)** _____ the school had established quotas for minority students was there any chance of being admitted. In some cases blacks were admitted **(4)** _____ they had scholarships. The Civil Rights legislation enacted in the 1950s and 1960s played a significant role in overcoming inequality and discrimination. Nevertheless, even today restrictions barring certain people have not been lifted from many private clubs. **(5)** _____ you are black or a woman there are still places—country clubs and club rooms especially—where you will not be likely to gain admittance. So exclusive are some of these clubs that **(6)** _____ you are a white man, you would be granted access **(7)** _____ you are a member and are wearing a suit and tie.

Flight Information

For domestic flights you should be at the airport one hour ahead of time **(8)** _____ you do not have any bags to check in, in which case you can turn up thirty minutes before the scheduled departure. Once aboard the aircraft, you should put your carry-on bag in the overhead compartment **(9)** _____ it cannot fit beneath the seat in front of you. Thanks to the efficiency of computer networks, your travel agent can give you your seat assignment and boarding pass in advance but **(10)** _____ you purchase your ticket more than two weeks before departure. Unfortunately, once your ticket has been made out, you cannot change your return flight **(11)** _____ you pay a penalty.

Exercise 2 *(Focus 2)*

Express these statements from an automotive manual more emphatically by beginning the sentence with *only if* or *not unless*. Make any other changes you think are needed.

E X A M P L E :   You should use the jack to change a flat tire only if your vehicle is on flat ground.

Not unless (or **Only if**) *your vehicle is on flat ground should you use the jack to change a flat tire.*

1. Your engine will not run smoothly unless you change the oil regularly. _____

_____

2. The treads of your tires will wear evenly only if you keep the tires properly inflated. ___

_____

3. You need to add special antifreeze solution to your windshield washing fluid if you live in a climate where temperatures drop below freezing in the winter. _____

_____

4. When checking transmission fluid, you will obtain an accurate reading on the level gauge only if the temperature of the fluid is between 60 and 80°C. _____

_____

5. Your vehicle will not be able to run on leaded gasoline unless it was made prior to 1980.

_____

Exercise 3 *(Focus 3)*

Complete each of the blanks by forming a negative conditional statement with the cues in parentheses, which give conditions that are contrary to fact. Use *if . . . not* or *unless* as appropriate. In cases where both are possible, use *unless*. Add any words or phrases you think are needed.

E X A M P L E :   Some months ago, the former Administrative Assistant warned Terry, who was about to take over her job, that she would have trouble keeping track of the reference books circulating in the department. Terry is pleased that she compiled a database of all the reference books because_____.
(do so/not know where the books were)

Completion: *unless she had done so, she wouldn't know where the books were.*

1. Maria is having an easy time revising her essays this semester. She is happy she learned how to use the computer because_____

_____.

(not know word-processing/have to spend a lot of time re-writing)

2. This morning I received an urgent letter from an environmental organization looking for my support. It says that_____

_____.

(not stop the timber industry/virgin forest be destroyed)

3. When I saw her yesterday, my friend, Gertrude broke the bad news of her having been turned down once more after a job interview. Gertrude wondered whether "honesty is the best policy" was the best maxim in helping one obtain a job. Actually_____

_____.

(not be so frank and outspoken/get the job she wanted)

4. Richard is going to France this summer and feels confident and excited. He told me that

_____.

(not find someone to practice French with/not feel so confident)

5. My grandparents came from Russia and never really learned to speak English well, and I never learned much Russian. Now that they are gone I really regret this because_____

_____.

(not speak only English/understand more about grandparents)

6. It's not difficult to discover one of Virginia's passions. Go into her apartment and you'll see tapes and CDs all over the place._____

_____.

(not such a great music-lover/not have so many tapes and CDs)

7. Most people admit that violent crime is a major problem. Although the gun lobby feels otherwise, many believe that _____

_____.

(be harder to get a gun/number of murders decrease)

8. Tony has been feeling sick for the last two weeks. His friends have been urging him to make an appointment to see a doctor._____

_____.

(have health insurance/go to see a doctor by now)

9. The south of the country has been experiencing drought conditions. Farmers are worried because_____

_____.

(be rain soon/crops be ruined)

Exercise 4 (Focus 4)

Choose the correct form–*even though* or *even if*–for each blank.

1. _____ he is confined to a wheelchair and is deprived of speech, the British astrophysicist, Stephen Hawking, has made major contributions to our understanding of the universe.

2. Speak to any successful writer about finding a publisher; he or she will tell you that you've got to keep trying _____ you receive a hundred rejections.

3. Because of his good sense of humor, his wonderful ability to mimic, and his dramatic use of gestures, my friend Sam makes himself understood no matter where he travels _____ he speaks no more than a few words of any foreign language.

4. During the Great Depression of the 1930s, many people, _____ they had college degrees, wound up having to scramble for whatever work they could get. My grandfather, for example, sold leather belts on streetcorners for a time.

5. I am utterly amazed that she still smokes _____ her uncle who was a heavy smoker recently died of emphysema.

6. When my great grandmother was growing up, she lived on a farm and everyone in her family had to rise early in the morning _____ it was cold and dark and they were still tired.

7. _____ he had a good lawyer and a plausible alibi, the defendant was found guilty by the jury and sentenced to a prison term.

8. Along with Henry David Thoreau and John Muir, Aldo Leopold is among the most frequently quoted authors in conservation circles today, _____ the public has had limited access to his work.

9. The Victorians found it impossible to dismiss Darwin _____ many were repelled by his ideas that we share a common ancestor with the apes.

10. In a democratic society, people must accept the decision of the majority _____ it runs contrary to how they voted.

Exercise 5 *(Focus 5)*

When made into complete sentences the information in the columns on the next page will be a list of travel tips about staying in London. Make advice statements by combining information in the Condition and Advice columns. Use an appropriate conjunction: *if, only if, unless, even if, even though.* Make any changes necessary. The condition statements can either begin or end your sentence.

Advice	**Condition**
1. Don't get on the tube in rush hour	a. You feel comfortable driving on the left
2. Take the river boat up the Thames to Hampton Court	b. You are a foreign visitor
3. Don't rent a car	c. You want a feeling of the countryside
4. Go to visit the Crown Jewels on a weekend	d. You're prepared to stand
5. Check to see that the flag is flying over Buckingham Palace	e. You want to know about the history of the city
6. Expect to pay 15% VAT (Value Added Tax) when you purchase anything except food or books	f. It's not your fault
7. Be sure to visit the London Museum at the Barbican	g. You have studied English in North America for several years
8. Be prepared to encounter accents and dialects that will perplex you	h. Your time isn't limited
9. Always say "Sorry" when you bump into someone	i. You want to know when the Queen's in residence
10. Take a stroll on Hampstead Heath, London's largest park	j. You don't mind waiting in line for at least an hour

1. _____
2. _____
3. _____
4. _____
5. _____
6. _____
7. _____
8. _____
9. _____
10. _____

Adverbial Clause
Reduction/Participles

Exercise 1 *(Focus 1)*

The following letter from your intrepid Aunt Nelly concerning her latest trek in the Himalayas contains a number of full adverbial clauses. Underline each of them and then rewrite the letter using the reduced form.

Greetings from the roof of the world!

   While I am waiting for a helicopter to arrive, I'm taking advantage of the time to write you a quick letter. Let me go back to the beginning. After we spent a couple of days in Kathmandu, we took a bus to a little village where our porters were assembled. It was wonderful to get on the trail. When we started out we were at a low elevation in a semitropical landscape, but the trail led ever upward, and in three days, we were among steep cliffs and towering mountains. I've never seen so many waterfalls. After we had trekked for a week, we came to the snow zone. I was glad I had brought a lot of warm clothes. The water in my canteen froze every night! Before we climbed the high pass, we had to stay in one place for a couple of days so we could get used to the high altitude. If you don't acclimatize you can get very sick. Even so, while I was huffing and puffing my way to the top of the pass, I had a headache and wobbly knees. But the pain was worth it. The view was spectacular—jagged peaks everywhere, like a frozen stormy sea.

   Unfortunately there was an accident on the way down. While he was scrambling over loose rock, Pete, a member of our party, fell and twisted his ankle. Luckily, the next village wasn't far. But Pete can't continue; his ankle is very swollen and he can't walk. We radioed for help and a helicopter is on the way. I'm sending this letter with poor Pete, so bye for now, and see you in a few weeks.

Nelly

P.S. Oh, I almost forget to tell you. Before I left the United States, I bought a pair of those hiking boots you recommended. They've been great.

_____

_____

_____

_____

_____

_____

_____

_____

_____

_____

_____

_____

_____

_____

_____

_____

_____

_____

_____

_____

_____

Exercise 2 *(Focus 2)*

Rewrite the following folk tale, transforming each full adverbial clauses into a reduced form.

Don't Count Your Chickens Before They Hatch

There once lived a woman called Johanna whose family were beekeepers. Because she wasn't very rich, she had to go to the market every year to sell the family's honey.

As she had a long way to go, she had a lot of time for her thoughts to wander. Along the road she walked, carrying the jar of honey upon her head. Because she was daydreaming, she began calculating the money she would get for her honey. "First," she thought, "since I will get a good price for the honey, I will buy eggs. The eggs I'll then set under my brown hens, and in no time, there will be plenty of little chicks. Soon they'll become plump chickens, and I'll sell them and buy lambs."

Johanna then began to imagine even grander things. "Because they love lamb so much, everybody will be willing to pay dearly, I'm sure. And since I'll make so much money, I'll soon be richer than my neighbors. That will be so wonderful. I can hardly wait to see the looks on their faces when they see me dressed in finery! And as I'll be rich and respected, I'll marry off my children to the wealthiest people in town!"

Trudging along in the hot sun, she could see her fine sons and daughters-in-law, and how the people would say that it was remarkable how well-off she had become, who was once so poor and low.

Because she was taking so much pleasure in her fantasy, she began to laugh gaily, and preen herself, when, suddenly, striking the jar with her hand, it fell from her head, and smashed upon the ground. The honey became a sticky, dirty mess.

Since she saw clearly now the ruin of her dreams, Johanna collapsed upon the ground and wept bitterly.

_____

_____

_____

_____

Exercise 3 *(Focus 3)*

The famous Sherlock Holmes and his assistant, Dr. Watson, put up for the night in an old hotel in the country. During the night, Watson tapped on Holmes' door to tell him he heard strange noises below. Suggest a reason (cause) for each of Holmes' actions by adding a reduced adverbial clause to each sentence below.

E X A M P L E :   Holmes got out of bed

Hearing someone at the door, Holmes got out of bed.

1. Holmes softly but quickly went down the stairs.

_____

2. Holmes inspected the room thoroughly.

_____

3. Holmes went to the window which he noticed was open.

_____

4. Holmes went out.

_____

5. Holmes shone his light into the bushes.

_____

6. A young boy trembled.

_____

Exercise 4 *(Focus 4)*

Fill in the following table with reduced adverbial or adjectival clauses. The first one has been done for you.

E X A M P L E :   *Hitting a reef in a storm,* the ship was destroyed.

Reduced Clause	Main Clause
1. _____	, the ship was destroyed.
2. _____	, a man floated in the ocean for a day.
3. _____	, he drifted onto shore.

4. _____, he thanked God for sparing his life.

5. _____, he found he was on a small island.

6. _____, he made a meal.

7. _____, he found some useful tools.

8. _____, he wondered who else was on the island.

Exercise 5 (Focus 4)

Match the following main clauses and participial phrases. Then, rewrite the two clauses, inserting the participial phrase correctly.

Participial Phrases

1. Rising 1,250 feet,
2. Considered by many to be the most beautiful building in the world,
3. Completed in 1914,
4. Extending over 1,500 miles,
5. Hoping to control floods, create new arable land, and supply electricity,
6. Used formerly for gladiatorial, wild beast, and other displays,
7. Derided by many when it was finished in 1889,
8. Named for Sir Benjamin Hall, commissioner of works in 1856 when the bell was installed,

Main clauses

a. the Great Wall of China, which was begun in the third century B.C., was not completed until more than a thousand years later.

b. the Coliseum in Rome was completed by the emperor Titus in 80 A.D.

c. the Eiffel Tower has become a beloved symbol of Paris.

d. the Empire State Building in New York City is one of the highest buildings in the world and a top tourist attraction.

e. Big Ben is the great clock tower of the Houses of Parliament in London.

f. the Taj Mahal in Agra, India, is a mausoleum built by Shah Jahan in the seventeenth century for his wife.

g. the Panama Canal allowed ships to pass between the Atlantic and Pacific Oceans without having to make the long journey around Cape Horn.

h. Egypt, with Soviet assistance, built the huge Aswan High Dam between 1960 and 1970.

_____

_____

_____

_____

_____

_____

_____

_____

_____

_____

_____

_____

_____

_____

_____

Exercise 6 (Focus 5)

Circle the correct option.

E X A M P L E : _____ by the unwanted attention, the young visitors could hardly wait
to leave the reception.

a. Embarrassing   (b.) Embarrassed

1. _____ the picnickers, the black flies buzzed round their heads.

   a. Annoying   b. Annoyed

2. The speaker, while _____ with his audience, continued to smile as he answered
their questions.

   a. irritating   b. irritated

3. _____ as the manuscript was, the scholars found it exciting.

   a. Puzzled   b. Puzzling

4. The child, _____ by the shadow on the wall, dove beneath the bedcovers.

   a. frightening   b. frightened

5. The tourists were utterly _____ in the railroad station by the crowds and the noise.

   a. confused   b. confusing

6. _____ by the title, Edmund decided to see the movie.

   a. Intriguing   b. Intrigued

7. _____ was how all of us had found the celebrated film.

   a. Boring   b. Bored

Exercise 7 *(Focus 6)*

Correct the dangling participles in the following sentences.

E X A M P L E : After working for hours, the garden looked beautiful.
After working for hours, Jane made her garden look beautiful.

1. Sniffing under the hedge, the man spotted an opossum.

   _____

2. Hoisted up to the fifth floor with a heavy rope, the movers brought in the piano through the window.

   _____

3. After hiking all day long, the thought of a tent and sleeping bag was very attractive.

   _____

4. The hunter shot the rhinoceros, while charging down on him.

   _____

5. Planted in the fall, she enjoyed the daffodils.

   _____

6. Racing down the highway because he was already late for work, the road seemed very long to Robert.

   _____

7. Putting on sunglasses, the glare wasn't so bad, he thought.

   _____

8. Frustrated by overly complicated questions, the test was infuriating.

   _____

Choose the <u>one</u> word or phrase that best completes the sentence.

1. _____ the treaty is ratified will the nation receive any agricultural assistance.
   - (A) Unless
   - (B) If
   - (C) Not only
   - (D) Not unless

2. _____, the arguments for the possibility of extraterrestrial intelligence can be summarized as follows.
   - (A) To summarize
   - (B) Shortly
   - (C) Briefly
   - (D) In briefly

3. _____, the medicine finally began to have some effect on the inflammation.
   - (A) Taking a tablet four times a day
   - (B) After taking a tablet four times a day
   - (C) After I took a tablet four times a day
   - (D) My taking a tablet four times a day

4. That store is always open 24 hours a day, _____ it's a national holiday.
   - (A) if
   - (B) even if
   - (C) even
   - (D) despite

5. The army would have surrendered _____ reasonable terms had been offered.
   - (A) unless
   - (B) even though
   - (C) even if
   - (D) if

6. The survivors of the crash, _____ close together for warmth, survived a freezing night on the side of the mountain.
   - (A) since huddled
   - (B) because huddling
   - (C) after huddled
   - (D) huddling

7. _____, apply a finish coat of polyurethane varnish to the wood after sanding lightly.
   - (A) Lastly
   - (B) The last
   - (C) Final
   - (D) In conclusion

8. _____ it was more or less guaranteed to be useful and profitable, the Edison Labs wouldn't have been interested in experimenting with a new idea.
   - (A) If
   - (B) Even if
   - (C) Not unless
   - (D) Unless

9. The street sweeper, _____ in abject poverty, ran after the man he saw drop his wallet.

   (A) living   (C) after living

   (B) lived   (D) though lived

10. After hypothesizing, the first thing is to observe and _____ to verify.

    (A) secondly is   (C) nextly is

    (B) the second thing is   (D) then is

Identify the one underlined word or phrase that must be changed in order for the sentence to be grammatically correct.

11. The bus <u>would not have crashed</u> <u>unless</u> the roads <u>had not been</u> icy.
              A   **B**   **C**   **D**

12. The language of the inscription was <u>bewildered</u> <u>even to</u> the team of <u>dedicated</u> specialists
                                     A   **B**   **C**

    <u>who had studied</u> historical dialects in the region for decades.
         D

13. The children <u>were not allowed</u> outside <u>on Saturday</u> afternoon <u>only if</u> they <u>had finished</u>
                 A   **B**   **C**   **D**

    their homework.

14. <u>There are</u> a number of <u>method</u> ballistics experts use <u>to determine</u> the angle of trajectory
     A   **B**   **C**

    <u>of a given projectile.</u>
    D

15. <u>In overall</u>, <u>as we have seen</u>, Ernest O. Lawrence's contribution to particle physics is
     A   **B**

    unquestionable, <u>even though</u> he did not live <u>to develop</u> the final stages of many of his
               C   **D**

    conceptions.

16. Because <u>having signed</u> the contract, the company knew <u>it would be</u> responsible
          A   **B**   **C**

    <u>in the event of</u> damages.
       D

17. <u>Irritating</u> by <u>the lack of</u> attention, the <u>frustrated</u> customer began <u>to shout</u> his demand
     A   **B**   **C**   **D**

    for a refund.

18. <u>In order to</u> separate the isotopes, follow <u>these steps</u>. <u>At first</u>, place the emulsion <u>in a</u>
     A   **B**   **C**   **D**

    vacuum chamber.

19. <u>Would</u> anyone, <u>even</u> in the brightest of circles, <u>have thought</u> such a solution possible
     A   **B**   **C**

    <u>only if</u> a mere five years ago?
     D

20. <u>Unless</u> it <u>weren't</u> for the two previous drought years, the reservoirs <u>would</u> now <u>be</u> at
     A   **B**   **C**   **D**

    capacity.

UNIT

18

Gerunds and Infinitives as Objects

Exercise 1 *(Focus 1)*

As you read the following text, circle all gerund complements and underline all infinitive complements. (Not every sentence may have one.)

America's Maverick Inventor, Thomas Edison

(1) Thomas Alva Edison, born in 1847, was America's most prodigious inventor, with over 1,093 patents to his name. **(2)** He was a mischievous and inquisitive boy who, at the age of six, set the family barn on fire, "just to see what would happen." **(3)** At school, he was unable to concentrate and was forced to leave because his teacher found him "addled." **(4)** His mother, a former teacher, began tutoring him at home and soon had him reading Shakespeare, Dickens, and Gibbon.

(5) At age 12, he launched his business career, hawking newspapers and sundries on the train that ran between his hometown and Detroit. **(6)** He set up a lab in a baggage compartment that caught fire one day when one of his experiments exploded. **(7)** He learned to operate the telegraph, and during the 1860s, he wandered the country. **(8)** He often neglected his duties to use the lines for experiments—and once blew up a telegraph station while tinkering with a battery. **(9)** He drifted to New York City, and before long, started to invent things. **(10)** When he was 22, he engineered his first successful invention, an improved stock ticker which could keep up with the frenzied speculation of the New York Stock Market. **(11)** Edison earned $40,000 for the invention and with that he began manufacturing telegraphic equipment. **(12)** His next major invention was the diplex method of telegraphy whereby one line could carry up to four messages at the same time. **(13)** Successful and finally established, with a lab of his own assistants, he devoted the rest of his life to experimenting and inventing.

(14) "Anything that won't sell, I don't want to invent," he said. **(15)** Not a scientist or thinker in the way that Newton or Einstein were, Edison cared little about advancing scientific knowledge. **(16)** Instead, he became absorbed in making marketable products and making them quickly. **(17)** Moving to a new "invention factory" (the first large-scale industrial research laboratory) at Menlo Park, New Jersey in 1876, he soon began taking out a patent a month. **(18)** Wax wrapping paper, the mimeograph machine, and a commercially viable telephone were some of the wonders that flowed from the cornucopia of Edison Labs.

(19) Edison was testing ways to record telegraph messages when he stumbled onto the principles of his most unique invention, the phonograph. **(20)** Before a few co-workers in 1877, he shouted "Mary had a little lamb" into an apparatus that looked like a small hand-turned lathe with a needle that scratched a groove in the tinfoil. **(21)** He then put the needle back in the starting position and a scratchy, squeaky nursery rhyme came back out of the machine.

132

(22) In 1878 Edison turned his attention to perfecting a safe and inexpensive electric light to replace oil lamps and gaslights. **(23)** He tried out numerous materials to see if they would carry a current and glow: coconut fibers, lamp wick, fishing line, even hairs from a friend's beard. **(24)** Finally he tried passing a current through a carbonized thread in a vacuum—and it worked. **(25)** No system existed to make and distribute electricity to the consumer, and so Edison went on to design a flurry of new products: screw-in sockets, light switches, insulated wire, meters, fuses, conductors, underground cables, a generator, and even the central power station. **(26)** In so doing, he changed forever the face of the American home and workplace. **(27)** The age of electricity was born.

(28) Oddly enough, in all his long and distinguished career, Edison made only one important scientific discovery, the Edison effect—the ability of electricity to flow from a hot filament in a vacuum lamp to another enclosed wire but not the reverse, but because he saw no use for it, he failed to pursue the matter. **(29)** He attributed his own success to sheer perseverance; in his own words, "Genius is one percent inspiration and ninety-nine percent perspiration."

Exercise 2 *(Focus 1)*

Complete the following sentences based on the passage in Exercise 1. Use *to*-verb or verb + *-ing*.

EXAMPLE: As a young boy, he liked *doing* things "just to see what would happen."

1. Edison's mother decided _____ him at home.

2. At age 12, Edison began _____ business on a train.

3. Experimenting, he caused a baggage car _____ fire.

4. Undaunted by accidents, he kept on _____ and succeeded in _____ a telegraph station.

5. In New York City, Edison managed _____ a machine which proved invaluable to the Stock Market.

6. With the invention of his stock ticker, Edison started _____ big money.

7. He hired a crew of technicians _____ for him at Menlo Park.

8. Edison's next major invention was the diplex method of telegraphy, which allowed one line _____ four messages at once.

9. Edison did not care about _____ things that wouldn't sell, nor was he concerned with _____ scientific knowledge.

10. In making the first phonograph, Edison learned how _____ sounds.

11. Edison hoped _____ oil lamps and gaslights with an inexpensive light bulb.

12. Edison did not delay _____ many new electrical products.

13. Edison's many inventions and conveniences encouraged the consumer _____ electricity.

Exercise 3 *(Focus 2)*

Read the following sentences. Write NO beside the incorrect sentences and make all necessary corrections.

EXAMPLE: <u>NO</u> Please don't forget ~~picking~~ *to pick* up the children after work.

1. _____ The movie was so good I couldn't stop to watch it.

2. _____ Did I mention my accepting their invitation to dinner?

3. _____ Jonathan can't stand eating in smoky restaurants.

4. _____ The ambassador assured the trade delegation that their country would continue benefiting from our technical assistance.

5. _____ I used to hate to eat meat when I was young but my parents forced me to.

6. _____ Madam, we regret to inform you that your dog has not been found.

7. _____ The crew failed to repair the hatch in time.

8. _____ Her lawyer advised her dropping the case.

9. _____ Thanks, a lot. I really appreciate your mention that to him.

10. _____ After he had shot his cousin by mistake, the hunter vowed never to touch a rifle again.

11. _____ Would you hesitate helping someone in need even if it would put your life at risk?

12. _____ God forbade Adam and Eve to pick any apples from a certain tree.

13. _____ The consultant urged them not to release the report until the latest figures were in.

14. _____ Gauguin hated to live in France and yearned painting on a warm and exotic Pacific island.

15. _____ The Senator reminded his secretary to cancel his appointment with the newsman.

16. _____ I don't deny to visit her but I advise you to stop questioning me about it.

17. _____ She appears having trouble finishing her report.

18. _____ Our biochemistry prof said he expected us putting in no less than six lab hours per week.

19. _____ I like to imagine him being happy, the way he was that enchanted summer.

20. _____ Another hurricane like the last one will cause this sea wall to collapse.

Exercise 4 (Focus 3)

A democracy is a form of government by the people either directly or through representatives. The majority of countries in the world today have some form of democratic government. A representative parliament, regular elections, universal suffrage, basic freedoms and rights are all hallmarks of a democracy. Write general statements about these ideas, using the prompts below. Include verb + -ing or to-verb in each response.

EXAMPLE: democracies   believe in   (power of the leaders is limited)
Democracies believe in the power of the leaders' being limited.

1. democracies   insist on   (holding free elections on a regular basis)
2. democracies   call for   (people vote whenever they want to determine the level of popular confidence in the present government)
3. candidates   argue about   (spend money for projects and programs)
4. voters   hope for   (elected officials do what they promised during their campaigns)
5. people   consent to   (accept the verdict of the majority)
6. people   complain about   (elected officials forget their promises)
7. elected officials think about   (get re-elected)

_____

_____

_____

_____

_____

_____

_____

_____

_____

Exercise 5 (Focus 4)

Complete the following dialogues with a sentence, using one of the following phrasal verbs and verb + *ing*.

carry on	look forward to
give up	put off
put up with	take up
go through with	cut down on

EXAMPLE: Don't you use salt any more on your food?

I've cut down on using salt after reading the latest medical findings.

1. I'm surprised to see you. I thought you were going to visit your parents this week.

   _____.

2. I can't believe that you're quitting your job. What's the problem?

   _____.

3. What are you going to do in France this summer?

   _____.

4. I thought your mother stopped that treatment a few months ago.

   _____.

5. Hey, George, old pal, what's up? Haven't seen you at the pub in ages.

   _____.

6. What are you doing now that your kids are away at college?

   _____.

7. You look tired. Didn't you get any sleep last night?

   _____.

Exercise 6 (Focus 5)

Read the following notes about important modern inventors. Write sentences about each person, using one of the following expressions: *be celebrated for, be famous for, be good at, be proficient in, be renowned for, be skillful in,* or *be successful in.*

EXAMPLE: Benjamin Franklin, American statesman, diplomat, and author (among other professions), invented the lightning rod, the Franklin stove, and bifocals.

Benjamin Franklin was an American statesman, diplomat, and author (among other professions) who was famous for inventing the lightning rod, the Franklin stove, and bifocals.

1. James Watt, Scottish engineer, invented the steam engine; coined the term, horsepower.

   _____

   _____

2. Robert Fulton, American inventor, improved the steamboat and the submarine; built twenty-one steamboats and encouraged the great era of steamboat travel but actually contributed more to submarine design.

   _____

   _____

   _____

3. Samuel Colt, American inventor and industrialist, pioneered mass-production techniques and the use of interchangeable parts; devised a single-barreled pistol with a revolving chamber so that a man could fire without reloading—the "gun that won the West."

   _____

   _____

   _____

4. Joseph Henry, American physicist and educator, guided others in research leading to famous inventions; he was first head of Smithsonian Institute; he advised and worked closely with Samuel Morse, inventor of the audible-signal telegraph, and Alexander Graham Bell, inventor of the telephone.

   _____

   _____

   _____

   _____

5. Enrico Fermi, Italian physicist, built the first nuclear reactor; did important research on atomic theory regarding the properties of metals and radioisotopes.

   _____

   _____

6. Count Ferdinand von Zeppelin, a German aeronautical engineer, perfecting the hot-air balloon and making it steerable with a gas engine to spin its props.

   _____

   _____

7. George Eastman, an American inventor and manufacturer, invented the Kodak camera, the first easy-to-use popular camera; perfected the processes for manufacturing dry photographic plates and flexible transparent film.

   _____

   _____

   _____

Perfective Infinitives

Exercise 1 *(Focus 1)*

Complete the blanks with perfective infinitives, using the verb in parentheses.

EXAMPLE: That is a fascinating topic for you *to have explored* (explore).

1. (a) Alan is glad _____ (join) the Peace Corps after having finished college. (b) His parents expected him _____
(go) to graduate school right away, but Alan was an idealist who also wanted to see the
world. On assignment to Tonga, he worked for two years helping to construct and improve houses. One of the things he learned to do particularly well was to make doors. (c)
He claims _____ (make) at least five hundred of them.

2. (a) _____ (dare) to dive from the cliff was something
my childhood neighbor, Joe, would always regret. He and I had been following a group of
older boys to one of their "hangouts" on a ledge over a shallow pond. We wanted to join
their club. (b) To become a member you had _____
(do) something risky. They told us to dive off and Joe did so without hesitation but he
twisted his back when he hit the water. The injury confined him to a wheelchair for the
rest of his life. (c) I have always considered myself lucky _____
(stay) put and not obeyed.

3. (a) Peter: "It was really nice of the Henderson's _____
(invited) us over." (b) Jane: "_____ (prepared) such a
spread was amazing. The hors d'oeuvres, the pasta, the breads, the salads, the pastries!
What a feast!" (c) Peter: "Everything was great. Still, _____
(eat) a bit less would have been better for me."

4. (a) I'm not so sure I would have like _____ (see) Pan-
dora's face when she opened the box. In the myth, Zeus warned her not to open the

box, but curiosity got the better of her. (b) _____
(resist) would have been impossible for someone so inquisitive. She peeped inside and out streamed all the evils that plague the world—sickness, age, every vice, and death. (c) It was good of Zeus _____ (put in) one last thing, however, and that was Hope.

Exercise 2 (Focus 2)

Which type of past meaning does each of the following sentences express: past relative to the present, to the past, or to the future?

1. Two years ago, Cynthia believed finishing her dissertation to have been a foregone conclusion. She had already done all the class and field work necessary. She was bright, energetic, had excellent organizational skills, and enjoyed writing._____

2. She was surprised when she became pregnant. The next nine months, though, turned out to be a rich time, one she was always very glad to have experienced. _____

3. But she had less inclination to spend long hours in the library or in front of a computer screen. Although she had intended to have finished more than half the writing by the time of the birth, she found herself unable to stick to her original plan._____

4. Her husband, Byron, was supportive throughout. He was there at the birth of their daughter, Reina, and has always considered it to have been one of the most moving moments he's known._____

5. In the first months after Reina's birth, Cynthia was too busy with her baby or simply too tired to write much, although she did manage a chapter. She figured that nothing else could have been done to have changed her output._____

6. Reina is nearly one and Cynthia has been quite pleased lately about Reina's having begun to have slept through the night._____

7. When Byron received a promotion recently, he and Cynthia arranged for a nanny to have been hired._____

8. With someone to help, Cynthia now expects to have made a lot of progress on her dissertation by the end of the year._____

Exercise 3 *(Focus 2)*

Restate the infinitives in the following quotations as perfective infinitives. Would you choose any for a personal motto or epitaph. Which?

E X A M P L E :   To doubt one's own first principles is the mark of a civilized man. (Oliver Wendell Holmes, American Supreme Court Justice)

To have doubted one's own first principles is the mark of a civilized man.

1.   To sin by silence when they should protest makes cowards of men. (Abraham Lincoln)

   _____

2.   To die for an idea is to place a pretty high price upon conjecture.
     (Anatole France, French author)

   _____

3.   There are two tragedies in life. One is not to get your heart's desire. The other is to get it. (George Bernard Shaw, British dramatist)

   _____

4.   To interpret is to impoverish. (Susan Sontag, American author)

   _____

5.   To be omnipotent but friendless is to reign. (Percy Bysshe Shelley, English poet)

   _____

Exercise 4 *(Focus 3)*

Who or what is the subject of each perfective infinitive clause below? Underline your choice.

1.   The motive appears to have been one of honor rather than passion.
2.   For so many people to have voted in the last election certainly makes questionable the claim that we have become indifferent about the democratic process.
3.   The fanatics believed themselves to have acted correctly despite the grief they caused.
4.   To have wasted so many taxpayer dollars is a scandal.
5.   Gretchen considers the president to have made the wrong decision in his choice of ambassador to Gabon.
6.   It was reputed to have been a stupendous discovery.
7.   Jean-Paul Sartre is considered to have been one of the most influential midcentury philosophers.
8.   Dr. Leakey considers this artifact to have arrived in the gorge at a later date.

Exercise 5 (Focus 4)

Rewrite each of the following clauses (*that*, *∅-that*, or *when* clauses) as a perfective infinitive clause. Make any word changes that are necessary.

EXAMPLE: José believes that he was misdirected by a sign that had probably been turned.

José believes himself to have been misdirected by a sign that had probably been turned.

1. Many people consider that America was discovered by Vikings.

_____

2. I'm glad I wasn't living in Paris during the Reign of Terror.

_____

3. The newpaper reported that the high government official had been selling secrets for many years.

_____

4. Fernando wishes he could have studied English in London when he was a child.

_____

5. Some people claim that the Nazca lines in Peru were made by extraterrestrials.

_____

6. Twenty-five years ago the number of sea otters was considered low enough that they were accorded endangered status.

_____

7. They promised that they would do all the work by Friday.

_____

8. Their teacher expects that they will check all their papers for spelling errors.

_____

9. She was thrilled when she was chosen to represent the class at the conference in Washington.

_____

_____

10. The guerrillas claimed that they were educating the people when instead they were terrorizing them.

_____

_____

Exercise 6 *(Focus 5)*

Rewrite each of the following sentences so that it contains a negative perfective infinitive clause. Use the pattern for formal written English.

E X A M P L E :   The boys never let me into their club, but I was always glad I hadn't jumped.
    *The boys never let me into their club, but I was always glad **not to have jumped.***

1. Jane: "What a feast that was!"
   Peter: "Groan. I only wish I hadn't eaten so much."

   _____

2. Roberto claimed that he had never heard of the assignment.

   _____

3. Before he saw the ghost, Scrooge was proud that he had never given a penny away.

   _____

4. Although, when the police stopped him, there was an open whisky bottle on the seat behind him and a very distinct smell on his breath, the driver of the car claimed that he had not had a drop all night.

   _____

5. Many leaders subsequently admitted that they had been wrong when they had not investigated the export of weaponry to belligerent nations.

   _____

Exercise 7 *(Focus 6)*

Use the cues on the next page to make sentences expressing a past wish that did not materialize or an unpleasant event that was avoided. Use the standard English pattern of *would like, would love, would prefer,* or *would hate* followed by a perfective infinitive. Make any changes that are necessary, including any needed verb tense changes.

EXAMPLE: do all my papers on a word processor
I would prefer to have done all my papers on a word processor.

1. have more time to use the swimming pool.

   _____

2. be discovered napping in class

   _____

3. be given a take-home exam.

   _____

4. spend longer with my classmates in the cafeteria.

   _____

5. come down with the flu during the lesson on perfective infinitives.

   _____

6. be able to use a Macintosh computer.

   _____

7. know how to add graphics to my reports.

   _____

8. be served coffee or tea in class.

   _____

9. do even more grammar exercises on my own.

   _____

10. come to class by mistake when it was a holiday.

    _____

Exercise 8 (*Focus 7*)

Write sentences with perfective infinitive clauses, using the cues. Use a variety of structures. If you wish, add descriptive words or phrases to expand the sentence.

EXAMPLE: Be wonderful . . . spend a month in Hawaii
It must have been wonderful to have spent a month relaxing in Hawaii.

It was absolutely wonderful to have spent an entire month in Hawaii, surfing, kayaking, and taking hikes on Kauai.

1. Be a miracle . . . escape alive.

2. Be sweet . . . send a cake and a gift.

3. Be shocked . . . read about the latest scandal.

4. Be generous . . . spend time doing volunteer work.

5. Be unacceptable . . . come to the event in old clothes.

6. Get together . . . be marvelous. (Start with *for* + noun)

7. Be tedious . . . work on an assembly line.

_____

_____

_____

8. Be thrilling . . . hang-gliding.

_____

_____

_____

Exercise 9 (Focus 8)

Make up sentences with _appear_ or _see,_ followed by a perfective infinitive for each of the following situations.

1. You are stopped on the road by a police officer. He asks to see your driver's license. You look for your wallet and can't find it. Give an appropriate response.

_____

_____

2. You go with a couple of friends to a rock concert. The lead singer is slurring his words, crashing into the guitarists, and falling down on the stage. You make a comment to your friends.

_____

_____

3. You are in a restaurant with your family. The waiter brought you your menus ten minutes ago and has not returned to take your order. You make a comment.

_____

_____

4. You are a teacher. A student hands you a paper done on the computer but the print is very faint and barely legible. Make a comment to her.

_____

_____

5. You are in a hotel. You have asked for a nonsmoking room. You go to the room given you and find there are ashtrays in several places and cigarette burns in the bathroom. You return to the reception. Make an appropriate response.

_____

_____

Exercise 10 (*Focus 9*)

You are a student at a job interview and are being asked the questions below. Respond using the same main verb. Use a phrase indicating time and add a perfective infinitive and any information you feel is appropriate.

1. What courses do you expect to have finished by June?

   _____

   _____

2. What, other than academic coursework, do you plan to have done before you graduate?

   _____

   _____

3. What other companies do you intend to have visited before you make a job commitment?

   _____

   _____

4. Was there ever a time when you were supposed to have done something but found yourself unable to because of some reason?

   _____

   _____

5. What do you hope to have accomplished within the next five years?

   _____

   _____

Exercise 11 (*Focus 10*)

Use the phrases below to create sentences about past possibilities, using perfective infinitives.

E X A M P L E :   weather...hot enough

   The recent weather was hot enough to have made me want to move to a place with a more moderate climate.

1. drank enough coffee

   _____

2. movie...scary enough

   _____

3. slide show...boring enough

   _____

4. storm . . . snowy enough

_____

5. be tired enough

_____

6. salesman . . . convincing enough

_____

Exercise 12 *(Focus 10)*

The following sentences express disbelief about an event or explain why something didn't happen. Combine the ideas in each pair of sentences into one sentence, using a perfective infinitive clause.

E X A M P L E :   The plants in the garden couldn't have survived. It was too cold last night.
   It was too cold last night for the plants in the garden to have survived.

1. Derek couldn't have gone to see such a frivolous show. He's too serious.

_____

_____

2. Dr. Mayer wouldn't return his students' essays without comments and corrections. He's far too dedicated a teacher.

_____

_____

3. They couldn't have slipped the guns through. The border's too well guarded.

_____

_____

4. That lawyer couldn't have lost the case. His arguments were too convincing.

_____

_____

5. We couldn't have believed his excuses. They were somehow too contrived.

_____

_____

UNIT
20 Adjectival Complements in Subject and Predicate Position

Exercise 1 *(Focus 1)*

In the following short texts, complete the adjective complements.

EXAMPLE: An abandoned and abused Scottish terrier named Bobby kept vigil for 14 years at the grave of a man who just before he died had given the animal a simple meal of scraps. That Bobby *could have been so dedicated* was remarkable and touching.

1. In 1975 a shipwreck victim off the coast of the Philippines spent two days on the back of a giant sea turtle who, during that time, swam on the surface of the water and did not even dive to feed itself. Turtles typically spend most of their time underwater. For a turtle _____ is unbelievable.

2. In 1950, in Hermitage, Tennessee, a very old woman named Aunt Tess suffered a bad fall at home and would have died but for her canary, who flew to the neighbor's home and beat her wings frantically on the window until she got attention. The canary then dropped dead of exhaustion. A bird's _____ is amazing.

3. A captive lady elephant, known as Bertha, lived for years in her trainer's room and didn't smash any of the furniture, even the cabinet where she knew her favorite foods were kept. That _____ is astonishing.

4. Chicken in poultry factories routinely have their beaks cut so they will not be able to inflict harm on each other in their crowded conditions. That _____ is disturbing when you really think about it.

5. A German shepherd missed his companion, who had moved from Brindisi to Milan, Italy, and left him behind. He set out on a journey of 745 miles and found his old master. For the German shepherd _____ is truly extraordinary.

6. Insects are great masters of disguise. Bugs can resemble thorns; butterflies, with wings closed, can resemble dead leaves; moths can look like patches of lichen; and there is a caterpillar in Costa Rica which has a pattern on its rear end that makes it look like a tiny viper. Insects _____ is remarkable.

Exercise 2 *(Focus 1)*

Imagine that you are again at various previous stages of your life. What would make you *happy*, *eager*, *anxious*, or *ready*? Write your answers in first person and use one of the adjectives listed above.

E X A M P L E :   baby

> I would be *eager* for my parents to play with me.
> I would be *happy* to splash in the bath.

1. baby	3. 5-year old	5. 10-year old
2. toddler	4. young teenager	6. late teenager

Exercise 3 *(Focus 2)*

Comment on the following facts found in the *Guinness Book of World Records* (McFarlan et al., New York, Bantam Books, 1989) using a *that* clause in subject position.

E X A M P L E :   The most expensive sport shoes obtainable are mink-lined golf shoes with 18-carat gold embellishments and ruby-tipped gold spikes by Stylo Matchmakers International Ltd. of Northampton, England, which retail for $17,000 per pair.

> *That someone would spend so much money on a pair of shoes is absolutely unbelievable.*

1. Emperor Bokassa of the Central African Empire (now Republic) commissioned pearl-studded shoes from the House of Berluti, Paris for his self-coronation in Dec. 1977 at a cost of $85,000.

   _____

   _____

2. The largest collection of valid credit cards contains 1,199 cards, all different, by Walter Cavanagh of Santa Clara, California (known as "Mr. Plastic Fantastic"). He keeps them in the world's largest wallet, 250 feet long, weighing 35 lb., worth more than $1.4 million in credit.

   _____

   _____

3. An unnamed Italian industrialist was reported to have lost $1,920,000 in five hours at roulette in Monte Carlo, Monaco, on March 6, 1974.

   _____

   _____

4. If meanness is measurable as a ratio between expendable assets and expenditure, then Henrietta (Hetty) Howland Green (1835–1916), who kept a balance of over $31,400,000 in one bank alone, was the all-time world champion. She was so stingy that her son had to have his leg amputated because of the delays in finding a *free* medical clinic. She herself lived off cold oatmeal because she was too thrifty to heat it. Her estate proved to be worth $95 million.

   _____

   _____

5. The highest death toll in modern times from an earthquake has been in the Tanshan earthquake (magnitude 8.2) in eastern China July 27, 1976. A first figure published Jan. 4, 1977 revealed 655,237 killed, later adjusted to 750,000. On Nov. 22, 1979, the New China News Agency unaccountably reduced the death toll to 242,000. As late as Jan. 1982, the site of the city was still a prohibited area.

   _____

   _____

Exercise 4 *(Focus 2)*

Consider each of the following nouns and determine one characteristic which would be odd/surprising/unexpected/impossible/strange (or an adjective of your choice) about the noun if it were true or if it had been true.

E X A M P L E : women

> *Women smoking cigarettes in public one hundred years ago would have been odd.*
> Or: *Their smoking cigarettes in public one hundred years ago would have been odd.*

1. men	6. a movie star
2. a workaholic	7. doctors
3. The President of the United States	8. the Mongol hordes
4. New York City	9. Donald Trump
5. airlines	10. Ernest Hemingway

Exercise 5 *(Focus 2)*

Read the following extracts from "The Daily Diary of Environmental Happenings" for the months of February and March 1993 (from *Buzzworm* magazine). Then create dialogues with the facts using a *that* clause and the adjectives provided.

E X A M P L E : frightening   Q: What's so frightening?

A: It is frightening that our nuclear power stations are so unprotected.

| 1. frightening | 3. unfortunate | 5. shocking |
| 2. fortunate | 4. encouraging | 6. good |

February 7: Middletown, PA—An intruder crashed his car through a gate and spent four hours hiding inside the Three Mile Island nuclear power plant before he was arrested, authorities said. "Nuclear plants are supposed to be able to protect against terrorists armed with high-accuracy weapons who have insider help," said Robert Pollard, a nuclear safety engineer. "This guy drives into the plant and they can't find him?"

_____

_____

February 12: Boston, MA—A prominent AIDS researcher told the annual meeting of the American Association for the Advancement of Science that as many as 1 billion people may be infected with AIDS, worldwide.

_____

_____

March 19: Amsterdam—A Japanese-owned tanker ship carrying toxic chemicals exploded in the North Sea, killing at least one crew member. Flames as high as 160 feet shot from the ship, a Dutch Navy official said. Authorities said there were no immediate reports of toxic chemical leaks.

_____

_____

March 20: Washington, D.C.—A U.S. attack submarine and a Russian missile-carrying sub collided under the surface of the Arctic Ocean. Neither submarine sustained major damage, authorities said.

_____

_____

March 20: Baghdad—A UN chemical weapons specialist said Iraq has destroyed about 70 tons of nerve gas and about 400 tons of mustard gas, as ordered by the United Nations.

_____

_____

March 24: Los Angeles, CA—The Clinton administration has designated a small bird, the California gnatcatcher, a threatened species under the Endangered Species Act. Coastal, sage scrub ecosystems will be set aside from development to provide habitat for the bird.

_____

_____

Exercise 6 (Focus 3)

What would be unexpected or unusual for the following people to do? Write a sentence that expresses your idea.

E X A M P L E : a world-class athlete

For a world-class athlete to eat lots of junk food would be unusual.

1. carpenters	4. rednecks	7. ballerinas
2. scuba divers	5. vegetarians	8. computer programmers
3. critics	6. Buddhist monks	

1. _____

2. _____

3. _____

4. _____

5. _____

6. _____

7. _____

8. _____

Exercise 7 (Focus 3)

Circle the best option and explain your decision.

E X A M P L E : a. It is heartening for some fast food chains to stop using Styrofoam packaging.

　　　　　　　 b. It is heartening that some fast food chains have stopped using Styrofoam packaging.

　　　　　　　 (It is true that some fast food restaurants have stopped using Styrofoam)

1. a. It is a pity for rhinoceroses to be hunted for their horns.

　 b. It is a pity that rhinoceroses are hunted for their horns.

_____

2. a. In scientific surveys, it is important for animals to be monitored after they are tagged.

　 b. In scientific surveys, it is important that animals are monitored after they are tagged.

_____

3.   a. After the forest fire is out, it will be useful for the surviving creatures to be counted and noted.

      b. After the forest fire is out, it will be useful that the surviving creatures are counted and noted.

---

4.   a. For nuclear power plants to have lax safety standards would lead to a greater incidence of cancer.

      b. Nuclear power plants' having lax safety standards will lead to a greater incidence of cancer.

---

5.   a. It is amazing for butterflies to migrate vast distances.

      b. It is amazing that butterflies migrate vast distances.

---

6.   a. It is true for endangered wildlife from developing countries to be smuggled into the United States.

      b. It is true that endangered wildlife from developing countries is smuggled into the United States.

TOEFL® Test Preparation
Exercises · Units 18–20

Choose the <u>one</u> word or phrase that best completes the sentence.

1. It is fantastic _____ the lottery.

   (A) anyone's to win　　　　　(C) for anyone to win

   (B) anyone to win　　　　　　(D) for anyone winning

2. If we really want to get the grant, I suppose we'll have to put up with _____ numerous forms.

   (A) to fill out　　　　　　　(C) having filled out

   (B) filling out　　　　　　　(D) to have filled out

3. It is sad _____ of endangered species is a lucrative business.

   (A) to smuggle　　　　　　　(C) for the smuggling

   (B) about smuggling　　　　　(D) that the smuggling

4. His advisors convinced the Secretary of Defense not _____ the announcement until all the details had been worked out.

   (A) to make　　　　　　　　(C) to have made

   (B) making　　　　　　　　　(D) having made

5. We had to change our plans, because last weekend, with the temperature below 0° F, it was simply too cold for us _____ camping.

   (A) that we went　　　　　　(C) to have gone

   (B) that we had gone　　　　(D) for going

6. The old prospector claimed _____ the mine before the mining company got its permit.

   (A) to discover　　　　　　　(C) discovering

   (B) to have discovered　　　　(D) having discovered

7. _____ on my lawn seems like quite a remote possibility.

   (A) That an extraterrestrial landing　　(C) An extraterrestrial to land

   (B) For an extraterrestrial landing　　(D) An extraterrestrial's landing

8. The Vice President of Sales and Marketing convinced _____ the revolutionary new software even before all the bugs had been worked out.

   (A) the CEO to announce   (C) to announce
   (B) the CEO announcing   (D) announcing

9. Just as he was about to leave the house, Fred thought about the possible showers later in the afternoon and remembered _____ the bedroom windows.

   (A) closing   (C) close
   (B) to close   (D) to having closed

10. They sent us a letter saying they would have liked _____ to our party last week, but were unable to due to unforeseen illness.

    (A) to come   (C) having come
    (B) coming   (D) to have come

Identify the one underlined word or phrase that must be changed in order for the sentence to be grammatically correct.

11. The inventor Nikola Tesla quit <u>working</u> for Thomas Edison because <u>he believed him</u>
                      A   **B**
    to <u>have been cheated</u> out of a promised bonus <u>for having improved</u> Edison dynamos.
              C   **D**

12. As they <u>looked around</u> the exam hall, the teachers <u>couldn't help noticing</u> that the
          A   **B**
    students were anxious <u>for themselves</u> <u>to begin</u> the test.
                        C   **D**

13. <u>When</u> so many bridges <u>could have collapsed</u> this year is <u>not only</u> terrible, but pathetic,
     A   **B**   **C**
    <u>in light of</u> our industrial strength.
        D

14. When the board of trustees suggested <u>to raise</u> the tuition for the second time in
                                      A
    three years, several members of the administration <u>questioned how</u> the institution
                                                   B
    <u>was going to</u> continue <u>to attract</u> students from middle-income families.
       C   **D**

15. It is interesting <u>about</u> the emperors of ancient Rome were in the habit of <u>making</u> deities
     A   **B**   **C**
    out of personal favorites <u>who had died</u>.
                     D

16. According to a recent discovery <u>made by</u> researchers at Vienna University with an
                                 A
    electron microscope, the ancient Egyptians <u>appear</u> <u>using</u> silk almost 1,000 years earlier
                                          B   **C**
    than <u>once thought</u>.
         D

17. He considers <u>himself</u> <u>being</u> lucky <u>to have been</u> the only one in his family
                A   **B**   **C**
    <u>not to have caught</u> the flu this winter.
         D

18. When the ambassador's family <u>returned to</u> this country after several years <u>of living</u>
    A B
    abroad, I told them that it <u>must have been</u> exciting <u>to be meeting</u> so many interest-
    C D
    ing people.

19. <u>Although</u> he was fond of <u>acting and singing</u>, rather than playing music himself, the
    A B
    emperor Nero <u>is famous at</u> <u>having fiddled</u> while Rome burned.
    C D

20. The pet-importing company reluctantly agreed to <u>the government inspecting</u> of all of
    A
    the crates and cages in the warehouse <u>that had come in</u> from South America and Africa,
    B
    <u>even</u> the ones <u>that had already received</u> initial clearance.
    C D

Noun Complements Taking *That* Clauses

Exercise 1 *(Focus 1)*

Underline each noun complement. Circle the abstract noun that precedes it.

E X A M P L E : Several religions share (the belief) that a redeemer will appear at the end of a
time of turbulence to usher in a new age.

1. The fact that sodium chloride makes up about 85 percent of all minerals in seawater
   accounts for the saltiness of the seas.
2. The city council rejected the plan to construct a bypass.
3. Scientists believe the reason that Mars appears red is because the rocks on the surface of
   the planet contain iron and also because a curtain of fine dust hangs in the atmosphere as
   a permanent haze.
4. In 1915, Alfred Wegener proposed the theory that continents might have moved or
   drifted.
5. The proposal to ban the sales of assault weapons is anathema to the NRA.
6. Everyone at Bell Labs applauded the news that another one of their researchers had won
   a Nobel Prize.
7. You should be aware of the boss's tendency to say no when he hears a proposal for the
   first time.

Exercise 2 *(Focus 1)*

Summarize the information from the text by completing the statements which follow.

   (1) Without water there is no life, and it is mountains that are responsible for capturing,
storing, and delivering water to the lowlands. (2) Historically, the first cultures developed
along rivers, which were ultimately fed by the water that came from mountains. (3) The
cultures that have thrived for millennia along the Nile, for example, have depended on water
that originally fell as rain in mountains as far away as Ethiopia and Burundi. (4) Mediterranean
civilizations developed where the Apennine, Atlas, Pindus, Taurus, and other ranges collected
sufficient moisture.
   (5) Destruction of mountain habitat can produce disastrous results for communities and
whole regions as is apparent today in Madagascar, Haiti, and the Philippines where timber cutting and grazing have denuded the highlands. (6) Rain on barren hills gathers force with great
speed and can generate floods. (7) In addition, valuable topsoil quickly erodes and washes out

to sea, and silt may clog irrigation systems and foul drinking water. **(8)** Without vegetation in higher elevations to help retain precious moisture in the ground, water supplies may dry up in dry seasons.

(9) In the mountain ranges of the developing world it is, ironically enough, ambitious aid projects from the World Bank and/or other agencies that are threatening watersheds. **(10)** Development schemes involving heavy equipment and the creation of roads for logging and mining can deeply scar the land and precipitate erosion. **(11)** Dams can drown villages. **(12)** The toll in terms of disruption to the indigenous people can be severe as villagers are forced from their homelands and are often obliged to seek their livelihoods on unproductive slopes higher up or, abandoning the mountain region completely, in the teeming slums of polluted cities.

EXAMPLE: The fact that _mountains capture, store, and deliver much of our water_ has made them crucial to cultures and civilizations.

1. It is a fact that _____ can cause flooding below.

2. It is a sad thought that _____ to make way for a dam or other development project.

3. The reason that _____ is because there is no longer any vegetation higher up to help retain moisture in the ground.

4. The ironic revelation that _____ is rather shocking.

Exercise 3 (Focus 2)

Which sentence in each of the following pairs contains a noun complement? Circle your choice.

EXAMPLE: a. The request that we contribute more money was turned down.
b. The request that you submitted is under consideration.

1. a. She denied the allegation that her family could have had a few skeletons in the closet.
   b. She denied the allegation that the newspaper reported.

2. a. The advice that I invest my inheritance is a good one.
   b. The advice that the judge gave the new attorney was thoughtful.

3. a. Does anyone here believe the notion that the earth is flat?
   b. Does anyone here believe the notion that Russell brought up?

4. a. The time that he referred to was undefined.
   b. The time that he came to visit I will always remember.

5. a. The chairman made a statement that I couldn't hear.
   b. The chairman made a statement that future meetings would be held on Monday.

Exercise 4 *(Focus 3)*

The following paragraphs describe amazing facts about famous people. Make observations about each set of facts using a *that* clause following *the fact/idea/news* etc.

EXAMPLE: The great Austrian composer Mozart died at the early age of 35. He left behind over 600 works, including 50 symphonies, over 20 operas, nearly 30 piano concertos, 27 string quartets, 40 violin sonatas and many other instrumental pieces, some of which date from the time he was only four years old.

The fact that Mozart could have achieved so much in such a short lifetime is a clear indication of his genius.

1. On Christmas Day in 1871, Thomas Edison took time out from his busy inventing schedule to marry 16-year-old Mary Stilwell. He didn't take that much time, though. An hour after the service he was back at work in the lab solving a production problem.

2. The polio virus was responsible for crippling hundreds of thousands of people in the first half of the twentieth century. The epidemics, usually during warm weather, turned summer into a time of terror. Fear of contagion caused entire communities to be quarantined and thousands of people to cancel vacations. In 1955 the American scientist Jonas Salk created a safe and effective polio vaccine, and a massive public vaccination program was undertaken.

3. After the invention of the telephone, Alexander Graham Bell was acclaimed everywhere. He gave innumerable speeches and interviews and joined a multitude of organizations, enterprises, and scientific groups. Yet he was ill at ease in public roles and would often hide away to avoid social engagements. He would sometimes lock himself in a bathroom or even hide in an attic until someone ferreted him out.

4. Franz Joseph Haydn, often referred to as "the father of the symphony," wrote his famous farewell symphony as a gentle hint to his employer, a member of the aristocratic Hungarian Esterhazy family, that he and the orchestra needed a rest. As the music drew to a close, one musician after another set down his instrument and stole away until there were only two violins left.

5. It was a widely held belief among nineteenth-century intellectuals that the mind was controlled by reason. Sigmund Freud, the father of psychoanalysis, began his career as a student of hypnotism. His work with mentally traumatized patients and his investigation of dreams led him to the realization that the reasoning faculty had far less dominion over the self than was previously believed.

1. _____

_____

2. _____

_____

3. _____

_____

4. _____

   _____

5. _____

   _____

Exercise 5 *(Focus 4)*

The following text about toxic wastes contains too many *the fact that* clauses. Underline instances of the fact in the text. Then, cross out those that do not seem necessary or are incorrect.

(1) One irony of life in the 1990s is the fact that the healthy, robust athlete may actually be at greater health risk than the inactive person. **(2)** Individuals at all levels of serious exercise often overlook the fact that they may be taking greater risks than they ever imagined due to an unhealthful environment. **(3)** At least three circumstances are affecting the health of all of us, but because the athlete spends more time in these degraded conditions than the nonathlete, the exposure is greater and so is the risk. **(4)** The first area of concern is the effect of stratospheric ozone depletion, which allows more intense ultraviolet radiation to penetrate the atmosphere. **(5)** Each year in the United States, statistics show the fact that approximately 500,000 new cases of skin cancer are diagnosed, and about 70 percent are believed to be attributable to exposure of the skin to ultraviolet rays. **(6)** Most of us can avoid going outside for any length of time in the spring and summer months between 10:00 A.M. and 3:00 P.M. when the sun's rays are the strongest, but this is not the case for professional athletes. **(7)** In addition to skin cancer, it is now known the fact that cataracts can develop and the immune system can be weakened, which might decrease immunity against infectious diseases. **(8)** The fitness enthusiast is especially affected by air pollution, the second area of concern, because the quantity of air inhaled during exercise and the depth of inhalation into the lungs are significantly greater. **(9)** The American Lung Association states the fact that running in a typically polluted urban area for 30 minutes is equivalent to smoking a pack of cigarettes a day. **(10)** A third area of environmental impact on athletes is that of pesticides and toxic chemicals used on athletic turf, from baseball fields to golf courses. **(11)** Luscious green turf disguises the fact that as much as nine pounds per acre of insecticides, herbicides, and fungicides—all of which can interfere with the human nervous system—lie upon and beneath the visually attractive surface. **(12)** Instead of stopping us from playing and working out, this information should give us the determination and incentive to stop the problems. **(13)** Given the state of our environmental knowledge, we must accept the fact that we must now protect ourselves with creams, sunglasses, hats, and by changing our outdoor exercise schedules, but ultimately, and even more importantly, we must get to the root of the problems and try to effect a change.

Exercise 6 *(Focus 5)*

Consider the situation of the Martinez family. Carlos and Teresa have four children, Jorge (18 years old), Gloria (16), Guadalupe (13), and Julio (9). The parents have worked hard to provide a nice home and a good education for all of the children. The children have all done well in their schoolwork, particularly Jorge, who is the apple of his parents' eyes and an honor student who has just received two scholarship offers for college. Jorge himself can hardly wait to leave the tiny home where he has grown up. The brothers share one small room and so do the sisters. Julio chatters a lot and leaves toys and clothes everywhere. The girls are very different from each other. Gloria likes boys with fast cars and Guadalupe likes to read, go to church, and talk to her friends on the phone. The children have frequent arguments. Comment upon the circumstances of the Martinez family using the words below and the *fact/idea/news* etc. *that* clauses.

EXAMPLE: Carlos and Teresa (proud of)

Carlos and Teresa are proud of *the fact that all of their children have succeeded in school*.

1. Carlos and Teresa (accustomed to)

_____

2. Jorge (excited about)

_____

3. Jorge (put up with)

_____

4. Gloria (jealous of)

_____

5. Julio (thrilled about)

_____

6. Guadalupe (concerned about)

_____

7. Gloria (annoyed with)

_____

Exercise 7 *(Focus 5)*

Suppose you saw people doing the following strange actions. What would you remind them of in order to help clear up their confusion? Write a sentence about what you would say.

EXAMPLE: walking on a golf course with bare feet

I would remind them of the fact that golf courses have high concentrations of toxic chemicals which could be dangerous to their skin.

1. forgetting to say "Thanks" when someone helps them or does them a favor

_____

2. lighting up a cigarette in a designated no-smoking area

_____

3. adding radiator coolant to the windshield fluid reservoir

_____

4. using an infinitive after "enjoy"

_____

5. neglecting to say "Excuse me" when they bump into someone

_____

6. going outside in thin clothing when the temperature is below 0°C

_____

7. driving 50 mph on a residential street

_____

Exercise 8 *(Focus 5)*

The following sentences review the structures learned in this unit. Correct those which contain errors. Write OK next to those that are correct.

E X A M P L E : The fact that she contributed so much to charity was laudable. *OK*

She wouldn't accept the notion which some kinds of cholesterol were beneficial to the body.

CORRECTION: She wouldn't accept the notion that some kinds of cholesterol were beneficial to the body.

1. The possibilities that arose from the new discovery were dazzling.

_____

2. What explains that in some cases the immune system turns against itself?

_____

3. The idea that Martians landed in his backyard.

_____

4. The news that the drought was over made some people careless in the way they used water.

_____

5. She was conscious of that they were both drifting apart.

_____

6. That disorder must be factored into equations and projections is commonplace in physics.

   _____

7. He is always boasting about that he has done two triathalons this year.

   _____

8. The notion that we are in full control of our minds is arguable.

   _____

9. There are some people who will never accept the notion which we are all born innocent.

   _____

10. That he could have gotten away with perjury is a sad comment on the justice system.

    _____

11. The committee supported that the institution had a lot to gain by extending health benefits to part-time employees.

    _____

12. The studies which we undertook led to greater understanding.

    _____

UNIT

22

Verbs, Nouns, and Adjectives Taking Subjunctive Complements

Exercise 1 *(Focus 1)*

Write a sentence that addresses the indicated situation using a verb of advice or urging + a subjunctive verb or *should* + base form. Use the verbs and objects in parentheses and add any other information you feel is relevant.

EXAMPLE: A wife to her husband about their son's expulsion from school. (urge/talk to principal)

She urges that he talk to the principal right away.

1. John to Bill about Bill's not being able to see the writing on the blackboard. (recommend/see eye doctor)

   _____

2. A group of citizens to the police chief about the rising crime in their neighborhood. (demand/assign police to their neighborhood)

   _____

3. Parents to their teenage daughter about when to get home after her date. (insist/get home by midnight)

   _____

4. A company memo to all personnel about wearing formal attire while on business trips. (stipulate/wear formal attire while on business trips)

   _____

5. Betty to her friend in a restaurant about the house special. (suggest/try)

   _____

6. The town planner to the town council about a traffic problem. (propose/ban traffic from the town center)

   _____

7. A math teacher to a student about some wrong answers. (advise/check figures)

   _____

8. A librarian to us about not being so loud. (request/lower our voices)

   _____

164

9. The president of the union to the workers about not losing hope. (insist /not lose hope)

_____

10. A mother to the judge about her son going to prison. (beg/not send her son to prison)

_____

Exercise 2 *(Focus 2)*

Imagine that you are having a conversation with your aunt Doris, a very concerned citizen, who is always phoning people and writing letters to magazines, newspapers, politicians, school principals, the police, etc. Write Doris' replies to your questions, using the prompts provided and a subjunctive complement.

EXAMPLE: What did the police chief say when you advised him to arrest all teenagers loitering in playgrounds? (ignore/advise)

He ignored my advice that he arrest all teenagers loitering in playgrounds.

1. What did the school principal do when you told him that he should ban pupils from chewing gum to and from school? (laugh at/suggestion)

_____

_____

2. What did the mayor say when you insisted on stores being closed on Sunday? (smile at/demand)

_____

_____

3. What did the editor say about your idea of not printing any story concerning sex or violence? (disregard/request)

_____

_____

4. What did your niece do when you told her she should forbid her children from watching cartoons on television? (not listen to/advice)

_____

_____

5. What did the president do in response to your letter about shutting down all weapons factories in the country? (ignore/plea)

_____

_____

Exercise 3 *(Focus 2)*

Imagine that your friend George has recently moved into a new house. Everything is fine except for one thing. The neighbors next door have a dog that annoys him very much. They leave it chained up on the deck and it barks all the time. George has already spoken to the neighbors once about this problem but they insist that their dog never barks. George has asked his friends what to do. Which advice of the friends was useful and which wasn't? Write a sentence that expresses your opinion of each friend's suggestion. Try to use as many advice or urging nouns as you can.

E X A M P L E :   Fred/call the SPCA (Society for the Prevention of Cruelty to Animals) and report the situation

Fred's advice that he call the SPCA and report the situation was sensible.

Friend	Advice
Fred	Call the SPCA (Society for the Prevention of Cruelty to Animals) and report the situation
Kurt	Poison the dog
Sally	Talk to the dog's owners again
Lisa	Make friends with the dog
Rod	Release the dog from the chain
Scot	Buy earplugs
Kate	Get other neighbors to sign a petition

_____

_____

_____

_____

_____

_____

_____

_____

_____

Exercise 4 *(Focus 3)*

Part A. The information below is made up from a doctor's notes. Fill in the following statements with *that* clauses containing subjunctive verbs.

E X A M P L E : It is advisable *that Ramona T. get an X-ray.* (Ramona T.)

Patient	Complaints/ Symptoms	Habits	Recommended Course of Action
Peter S./43	Bad cough; difficult breathing; halitosis	Smokes heavily	Take cough suppressant; stop smoking
Ramona T./52	Painful swollen fingers	Eats lot of sweets	Get X-ray; take Advil
Greg A./29	Pain in knees	Jogs 10 miles per day	Apply cold pack
Louise M./25	Nausea, fatigue	Perfectionist (newly married)	Pregnancy test
Matthew L./62	Severe chest pains; facial discoloration; gasping	Eats fatty foods	Immediate hospitalization
Ronnie P./38	Insomnia	Drinks lots of coffee; watches late night TV	Take tranquilizer
Samantha C./11	Itchiness/rash on legs	N/A	Apply cortisone cream
Corrine D./31	Fever alternating with chills/red watery eyes	Reads one novel a week	Flu medication; rest
James H./45	Headaches/ spaciness/shaky hands/yellow eyes	Drinks heavily	Cut down on drinking; take vitamin supplements
Eleanor K./27	Depression/skin lesions	Unknown	Blood test

1. _____ is vital. (Matthew L.)

2. It is essential _____. (Peter S.)

3. _____ is necessary. (Louise M.)

4. It is important _____. (Greg A.)

5. It is desirable _____. (Ronnie P.)

Part B. Create five sentences of your own with information from the chart on the previous page.

1. _____

2. _____

3. _____

4. _____

5. _____

Complex Passive and Raised Structures

Exercise 1 *(Focus 1)*

The columns below have information about old British superstitions related to animals. Match the descriptions in the first column to the results in the second column to form superstitions. Then make a statement for each match, using a complex passive.

EXAMPLE: *It is believed that if you see a hare at the outset of a journey, the journey will not go well.*

1. if a toad crosses your path
2. if a cat sneezes
3. if a lizard crosses the path of a bridal procession
4. if you see a golden butterfly at a funeral
5. if a weasel squeals
6. if a beetle crawls out of your shoe
7. if a spider falls on you from the ceiling of a house
8. if you chop up horsehair, spread them with butter on bread and feed them to your children

a. you will have longevity
b. bad luck will come to you
c. a death is imminent
d. you will have good luck
e. a legacy will come your way
f. your children will do well in school
g. the marriage will have problems
h. it will rain

Exercise 2 *(Focus 1)*

In the following passage, identify the complex passive sentences. Underline the main clause passive verbs. Circle examples of introductory *it*. Bracket [ ] the complement introducer *that* or *to*.

Folk Customs and Lore: Doors to Mysterious Britain

(1) There is always more to a nation than what we read in standard history books or economic surveys. **(2)** Folk customs and lore are especially rich sources of information that give us a certain "feel" for a place, a people, and the past, and restore a sense of wonder generally missing in observations restricted to "the hard facts." **(3)** Britain, because of its antiquity, is fertile ground for study. **(4)** Add to this a certain endearing eccentricity of character and what some would call "a haunted geography" and you have the promise of some intriguing revelations.

(5) Take, for example, the Furry Dance at Helston in Cornwall, which is held annually on May 8th. **(6)** It is reputed to be one of the oldest examples of a communal Spring festival dance still surviving. **(7)** It is claimed that the dance has been performed without a break, except in times of war and pestilence, since pre-Christian times. **(8)** According to one local legend, however, the dance is said to commemorate the victory of St. Michael the Archangel over the Devil in a struggle for possession of the town. **(9)** Today the dancing begins at six in the morning with the town band parading through the streets followed by all the children. **(10)** It is considered appropriate for everyone to participate, and at noon, the mayor, wearing his chain of office, leads all the townspeople who dance through all the main streets, and into gardens, shops and houses, in at one door, and if possible out through another, to bring the luck of Summer to the owners and tenants, and drive out the darkness of Winter.

(11) It is known that many customs have vanished since the industrial revolution, including one called Barring-Out the Schoolmaster, which was believed to have taken place at varying times during the year and in many parts of Britain. **(12)** On the appointed morning, the children locked the schoolmaster out of his own school, and refused to let him in until he had granted a holiday for that day, or according to some of the earliest accounts, he had promised a number of holidays during the coming months. **(13)** All his attempts to enter were fiercely resisted, and while the siege continued, it is said that the defenders shouted or sang traditional barring-out rhymes.

(14) Every land has its share of ghost and spirit lore but it is conjectured that Britain is the most haunted of them all. **(15)** Some spirit visitations are relatively benign, others grim. **(16)** It was recently reported that on the grounds of Holland House in the heart of London a headless ghost (presumably the first owner's son-in-law who was beheaded during the Civil War) was seen walking in the moonlight. **(17)** Holland Park in which the house stands also has its mysteries, and it is said that people have seen their doubles there. **(18)** (Traditionally, to see one's double warns of impending death within a year.) **(19)** In Glencoe, in the Scottish Highlands where a ghastly massacre took place in 1692, many people claim to have felt a brooding presence, a palpable oppression, and to have heard the sounds of sword against shield, faint cries, far-off moans, and calls for vengeance.

(20) It is supposed that belief in the existence of fairies was still strong among the country folk of Britain until quite recently, and there are many stories telling of their subterranean palaces, their hard-working helpfulness, and their love of music, dancing, and mischief. **(21)** Humans were thought to have been lured into their fairylands, there to be entertained for what seemed a short while, only to find on returning home that a hundred years of our time had passed. **(22)** Stories are common of youths who, having passed a night or two in fairyland, return to find their poor cottages tall mansions, and their lord's castle an ivy-clad ruin, and who, while conversing with their great grandchildren, suddenly crumble into a heap of ashes.

(23) Though it is undoubtedly true that many a folk custom has not found its way into actual practice in the twentieth century, many still remain. **(24)** And while we may take a lot of folklore with a grain of salt, it must be admitted that a good tale, full of surprise and mystery, is what we all like to hear.

170

Exercise 3 (Focus 2)

For each of the following numbered sentence groups, choose and circle the sentence that best fits the context, using the principles of presenting old and new information discussed in Focus 2. Consider each numbered group to be the beginning of a written article or spoken announcement.

1. It is believed that out of the roughly one hundred billion galaxies within range of our telescopes, each galaxy is home to a hundred billion stars.

   (a) It is surmised that half of these stars have planets.

   (b) Half of these stars are surmised to have planets.

2. (a) After many years as king of Athens, the ancient Greek hero, Theseus, was said to have lost the favor of his people and to have been forced to leave the city.

   (b) It is said that after many years as king of Athens, the ancient Greek hero, Theseus, lost the favor of his people and was forced to leave the city.

   He retired to the court of Lycomedes, king of Scyros, who at first received him kindly, but afterwards treacherously slew him.

3. (a) It was reported today that the space shuttle, Discovery, nearly lost power as it came in for a landing.

   (b) The space shuttle, Discovery, was reported to have nearly lost power today as it came in for a landing.

   A malfunctioning fuse was thought to be responsible.

4. In India, it is considered inauspicious to travel on either a Tuesday or a Saturday.

   (a) It is thought that the gods to whom those days are dedicated are tricksters quite capable of playing a prank upon vulnerable humans.

   (b) The gods to whom those days are dedicated are thought to be tricksters quite capable of playing a prank upon vulnerable humans.

Exercise 4 (Focus 3)

Imagine that you are a journalist being interviewed by a panel of students. The following are questions you have been asked about past, current, and future events. Give a response to each question by making a complex passive statement from the information in brackets: [ ]. Include an agent only if you think it is necessary. Try to use a variety of verbs.

EXAMPLE: Q: Why did they stop construction of the Black River nuclear power plant? [Inspectors thought the foundation was faulty.]

A: *The foundation was considered to be faulty.*
OR *It was considered that the foundation was faulty.*

1. Why is the senator from Kansas vacationing in New Hampshire? [The consensus is he will run in the primary elections.] _____

_____

2. Why has Congressman Loren not been seen for two weeks? [Word has it that he is undergoing treatment in a clinic in Arizona.] _____

_____

3. Why did the Rodax company take their new painkiller off the market? [They think the results of the lab tests were misinterpreted.] _____

_____

4. Why haven't we heard any more news about the Fisher case? [Most people guess it was settled out of court.] _____

_____

5. What's the latest update about the fire that burned down the Surf Hotel? [Police think it was the work of arsonists.] _____

_____

6. Is it true that we'll be seeing some new faces on the White House staff? [Our sources have it that there will be an announcement shortly about a major reshuffling.] _____

_____

Exercise 5 *(Focus 4)*

Here are some additional facts from *The World Almanac* and purported facts from "Harper's Index" (*Harper's Magazine*) and "Facts Out Of Context" (*In Context*, A Quarterly of Humane Sustainable Culture). Information considered to be a fact is indicated by (F); information thought to be possibly true is indicated by (?). Make up a complex passive sentence for each, using an introductory *it* + *that* clause. Then make a sentence for each, using a *to*-infinitive clause. Do any of your sentences sound awkward? Discuss your responses.

E X A M P L E : (?) Number of children admitted to hospital emergency rooms last year for injuries involving shopping carts: 32,866.

It is reported that the number of children admitted to hospital emergency rooms last year for injuries involving shopping carts was 32,866.

The number of children admitted to hospital emergency rooms last year for injuries involving shopping carts *is reported to have been* 32,866.

1. (?) There are approximately 75,000 edible plants found in nature. _____

_____

2. (?) Estimated number of birds that are killed in collisions with TV broadcast towers each year: 1,250,000. _____

_____

3. (F) Highest mountain in South America: Aconcagua, Argentina. _____

_____

4. (?) Number of Americans who do macramé: 6,500,000. _____

_____

5. (?) Estimated number of unsolicited phone calls made by U.S. telemarketers each second: 200. _____

_____

6. (F) Largest lake in the world: Caspian Sea. _____

_____

7. (?) Amount of time required to set the table for a banquet at London's Buckingham Palace: three days. _____

_____

8. (F) Longest undersea tunnel: the Channel Tunnel (between England and France). _____

_____

9. (?) Maximum fine for parking illegally overnight in Tokyo: $1,400. _____

_____

10. (?) Earth's population around 8,000 B.C., when farmers began harvesting domesticated plants: 4 million. _____

_____

11. (?) Number of people born every 10 days in 1991: 4 million. _____

_____

Exercise 6 (*Focus 5*)

Restate each of the (b) sentences below. Put focus on the subject of the *that* clause by raising it to the main clause and by changing the *that* clause to an infinitive clause. Use an appropriate infinitive form.

E X A M P L E : (a) Some superstitions involved doing things we would find disgusting today.

(b) For example, it appears that spiders and their webs were once swallowed whole as a cure for jaundice.

Restated: (b) *For example, spiders and their webs appear to have been swallowed whole as a cure for jaundice.*

1. (a) Coincidences often make us wonder if there is indeed a hidden plan at work in the universe. (b) Just months after the death of Galileo in 1642, it happened that Isaac Newton was born.

_____

2. (a) Gamblers are notoriously superstitious and take more than average care to avoid a run of bad luck. (b) It appears that the six most popular lucky objects carried around by gamblers at Monte Carlo are locks of hair, animal bones, holy relics, four-leafed clovers, hooves, and coins.

_____

3. (a) In Europe during the Middle Ages there was a curious belief that barnacle geese did not hatch out of eggs as birds normally do. (b) Instead, it seemed that the geese oozed out of old wrecks and planks along the shore.

_____

4. (a) The actress, Bette Davis, never performed publicly without her lucky charm, a gold beetle. (b) It seems that lucky charms give people a sense of confidence.

_____

5. (a) Bloodletting was a medical practice common up until the end of the eighteenth century. (b) It turned out that bleeding a patient to get rid of a disease was not a remedy at all.

_____

6. (a) "Fancy meeting you here" is an expression we use when we meet someone quite unexpectedly. (b) Last summer in Paris, I used the expression twice in one day when it happened that I ran into two people I hadn't seen for more than 10 years in different parts of the city.

_____

7. (a) Superstitions can be profitable to businesses as manufacturers and retailers of charms, amulets, and talismans know very well, but they can also have the opposite effect. (b) It seems that Friday the 13th accounts for an estimated loss of more than $300,000 because people choose to stay home rather than risk bad luck on this day.

_____

8. (a) One of the best known American superstitions, and one regularly reported in the media, is Groundhog Day on February 2. (b) If it happens that the groundhog sees his shadow, cold weather will persist for another six weeks.

_____

Exercise 7 *(Focus 5)*

Part A. The following drawings illustrate visual illusions. The sentences underneath them express the reality. State the illusion achieved by each, using *appears to be* or *seems to be*.

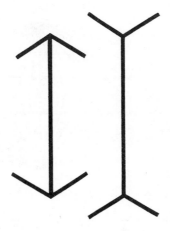

EXAMPLE: The vertical lines are of equal length.
Illusion: *The vertical line on the right appears to be longer.*
OR *The vertical line on the left appears to be shorter.*

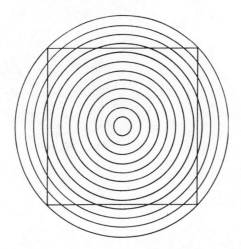

1. The square is a perfect square with straight sides.

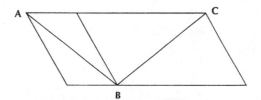

2. Lines AB and BC are of equal length.

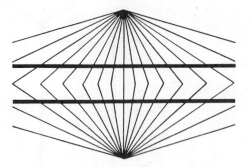

3. The horizontal lines are straight.

4. The circles that make up the figure are concentric and whole.

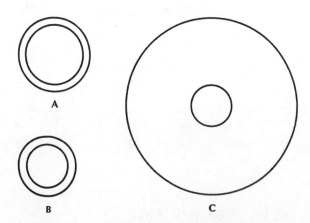

5. The inner circle of "a" and the outer circle of "b" are equal.

6. The inner circle of "b" and the inner circle of "c" are equal.

Part B. Look at the pictures below. Describe what you think each of them shows, using *appears to be* or *seems to be*. Compare your descriptions with others in your class to see if they differ.

7

8

7. _____

_____

8. _____

_____

Exercise 8 *(Focus 6)*

Ten people participated in a three-month seminar that promised to lower stress, improve self-esteem, unlock the secrets of creativity, and to help find the right job. A year after the seminar, a follow-up survey was undertaken to determine the effect of the seminar upon the participants' lives. The following chart gives facts about the participants at the time they began the seminar and one year later. Make up a sentence for each fact in the "One Year Later" column. Use a verb from the list below. Rephrase the information as necessary.

begin	proceed	grow	continue	fail
commence	come	tend	cease	

EXAMPLE: David began to feel positive about things.

Ron tended to remain critical of everything.

Participant	Beginning of Seminar	One Year Later
1. David	Negative attitude	Felt positive
2. Kit	Fear of nature	Appreciated nature
3. Ron	Critical of everything	Critical of everything
4. Ushi	Denied her impulses	Acted on many impulses
5. Anton	Poor listening skills	Valued other peoples' ideas and opinions
6. Holly	Conceded all arguments	Held her own in arguments
7. Glenn	Felt pent up and bored	Wrote a book
8. Heidi	Disliked working as nurse	Disliked working as nurse
9. Paula	Wanted to start own business	Business went bankrupt
10. Mario	Couldn't concentrate	Was steady and focused

1. _____

2. _____

3. _____

4. _____

5. _____

6. _____

7. _____

8. _____

9. _____

10. _____

Exercise 9 (Focus 7)

The following passage summarizes Paul Bowles' "Pastor Dowe at Tacaté," a classic tale of culture shock. First put [ ] around introductory *it* + *that* clauses and raised subjects + infinitive clauses. Then restate each introductory *it* sentence with a raised subject and infinitive clause.

EXAMPLES: (2) [The Indians who gathered to hear his first sermon seemed to be interested]

(4) [It appeared that Hachakyum was the Indian name for the great God] Hachakyum appeared to be the Indian name for the great God

(1) Pastor Dowe was a missionary newly arrived in a remote village in the jungle. (2) The Indians who gathered to hear his first sermon seemed to be interested, but when he had finished they silently drifted away. (3) Disappointed at the lack of enthusiasm, Pastor Dowe went the next morning to the hut of the headman, Nicolás, where he proceeded to engage in theological conversation. (4) It appeared that Hachakyum was the Indian name for the great god who had created the earth, the sky, and the Indians. (5) But to Pastor Dowe's dismay, it turned out that Hachakyum was not the creator of the white man nor of guns, illness, and difficulties. (6) That

178

was the province of another god, Metzabok. **(7)** Nicolás added that he knew Pastor Dowe had a phonograph and that no one would come to the service next Sunday unless there was music. **(8)** It happened that the only records Pastor Dowe had were big band dance tunes, which his deceased wife enjoyed. **(9)** He realized that if he failed to play this music, which he considered inappropriate, he would have no congregation. **(10)** On Sunday Pastor Dowe commenced to deliver his sermon but Nicolás demanded music first and all the Indians approved. **(11)** The following day Nicolás came to ask for salt, a request that the Pastor said he would think about. **(12)** Nicolás's daughter, a young girl named Marta, was playing with what appeared to be a doll, but when the Pastor inspected it, it turned out to be a baby crocodile swaddled in rags. **(13)** As the days went on, Pastor Dowe grew to wonder if he would ever succeed in his mission. **(14)** On a wet and foggy day, feeling the need to be alone, it happened that Pastor Dowe wandered away from the village. **(15)** After a while he met two Indians and they invited him to accompany them downstream on a raft. **(16)** It chanced that they brought him to a sacred place, where there were two caves in a towering cliff. **(17)** At the smaller of the caves the Indians asked Pastor Dowe to pray and he did so upon his knees. **(18)** They then proceeded to tell him that Metzabok was very happy now. **(19)** It proved to be a long tiring walk back to the village and Pastor Dowe collapsed into Nicolás's hammock which Marta gently rocked. **(20)** The next day was Sunday and it seemed that the whole village was gathered around the platform where the service took place. **(21)** Pastor Dowe read a psalm which he had translated using the names of Indian deities in place of Biblical names such as Jacob. **(22)** The people were pleased and while the music commenced to play and Pastor Dowe's servants distributed salt, Marta's crocodile crawled on the platform. **(23)** Nicolás then announced that he was giving Marta to Pastor Dowe as his wife. **(24)** The shocked pastor tried to refuse but noticing Nicolás's anger he took the little girl to his hut. **(25)** That night Pastor Dowe ceased to want to stay any longer in the village. **(26)** When it seemed that everyone was asleep, he took a small valise and slipped quietly and quickly away.

1. _____

2. _____

3. _____

4. _____

5. _____

6. _____

7. _____

8. _____

9. _____

10. _____

11. _____

12. _____

13. _____

14. _____

15. _____

16. _____

17. _____

18. _____

19. _____

20. _____

21. _____

22. _____

23. _____

24. _____

25. _____

26. _____

Exercise 10 *(Focus 8)*

Below is another set of superstitions. Each condition is separated from the result by a slash(/). A result considered certain (according to the superstition) is indicated by a plus sign (+). A result considered probable is indicated by a question mark (?). Make a sentence for each, using a raised subject. For results that are certain, use one of the following adjectives: *certain, sure, bound*. For results that are probable, use one of the following: *likely, apt,* or *liable*.

E X A M P L E :   (+) Eating sage/bring wisdom and strengthen the memory

Eating sage is sure to bring wisdom and strengthen the memory.

1. (?) Blonde-haired women/have more fun

   _____

2. (?) A man with hairy arms/grow rich

   _____

3. (+) Dew rubbed on sore eyes at dawn/take away tiredness, wrinkles, and pain

   _____

4. (?) Spitting on a coin you find/increase your wealth

   _____

5. (?) Crossing two knives on a plate after a meal/invite misfortune

   _____

6. (+) A tingling in the ears/indicate that someone is speaking ill of you

_____

7. (?) Throwing beans at a ghost/make it go away

_____

8. (+) A pregnant woman stepping over a grave/cause her child to die prematurely

_____

9. (+) Wearing a horsebrass/protect a horse from the evil eye

_____

Exercise 11 *(Focus 9)*

Complete the following sentences by inserting nouns, adjectives, and verbs from the lists below that fit the contexts. The first one has been done for you as an example.

Nouns	Adjectives	Verbs
superstitions	pleasant	watch
Yoga	useful	repair
police officers	marvelous	shop
National Parks	convenient	consider
English	tough	enforce
compositions	easy	write
silent movies	difficult	behold
malls	beneficial	understand
cars	amusing	hike
jokes	boring	learn
a child's progress		

1. _National Parks_ are _pleasant_ to _hike_ in if you are in adequate shape and the weather is nice.

2. _____ are _____ to _____
without the right tools.

3. _____ can be _____ to _____
if you want to stay supple.

4. _____ is _____ to _____
whether you are a parent or not.

5. Do you think that _____ are _____ to
_____ or do you think that they're entertaining?

6. Because of our largely scientific worldview, many _____ seem
_____ to _____ .

7. Most _____ are _____ to

   _____ if you don't get the punchline.

8. Quite a few _____ believe that vagrancy laws are not

   _____ to _____ .

9. Do you feel that _____ are _____ to

   _____ or do you think that your time could be better spent on

   other work?

10. _____ are _____ to _____

    in, if you know what you want and where to find it.

Exercise 12 (Focus 9)

Discuss with classmates answers to the following questions, giving your opinions and experiences. Use a "raised object" structure in your responses. An example is given for the first one.

E X A M P L E : Which things do you think are annoying to encounter?

To me, *traffic jams* are annoying to encounter.

1. In conversation, what subjects are always appropriate to mention?

2. In your opinion which sports are too dangerous to try?

3. Out of all the examples you've come across in this unit, which superstitions do you think would be interesting to discuss?

4. Which books have you found fun to read?

5. In your opinion which place is expensive to visit?

Choose the <u>one</u> word or phrase that best completes the sentence.

1. _____ quiet, alert, and patient is essential to anyone wishing to observe animal behavior in the wild.
   - (A) In order to be
   - (B) That a person is
   - (C) That a person be
   - (D) That being

2. In ancient Greece, _____ to have been the result of the Titan Atlas's adjusting the earth, which he kept propped up on his mighty shoulders.
   - (A) earthquakes were believed
   - (B) it was believed that earthquakes
   - (C) that earthquakes were believed
   - (D) they were believed the earthquakes

3. It is a fact _____ 10 major languages, led by Mandarin Chinese, English, Hindi, and Spanish, are spoken by more than 50 percent of the world's population.
   - (A) which
   - (B) that
   - (C) for
   - (D) of

4. At twilight the vision of diurnal fish _____ badly compromised by dim light, akin perhaps to the temporary blindness we face after walking from a sunlit street into a darkened building.
   - (A) has appeared
   - (B) it appears to be
   - (C) appears that
   - (D) appears to be

5. It was stipulated that a student _____ a grade point of not less than 3.0 in order to keep a scholarship.
   - (A) maintains
   - (B) maintain
   - (C) will maintain
   - (D) have to maintain

6. After the accident, he had to face up to _____ full recovery was going to take a long time.
   - (A) the fact that
   - (B) a fact that
   - (C) the fact of the matter
   - (D) that

7. We laughed when she told us she _____ any of the headlines of the tabloids at the supermarket checkout counters.
   - (A) does not tend
   - (B) tends to notice not
   - (C) tends not to notice
   - (D) never tends noticing

8. He ignored his doctor's recommendation _____ smoking cigarettes.
   - (A) about the stopping
   - (B) that must stop
   - (C) that he stops
   - (D) that he stop

9. The President _____ to be recovering quickly at Camp David, following a minor operation for the removal of a polyp.
   - (A) said the report
   - (B) the report is said
   - (C) reports
   - (D) is reported

10. _____ we are indeed living in the best of times may or may not be true.
    - (A) The fact
    - (B) The fact which
    - (C) That
    - (D) It is a fact

Identify the <u>one</u> underlined word or phrase that must be changed in order for the sentence to be grammatically correct.

11. The news <u>which</u> a new oil-indicating mineral called moganite <u>can be found</u> in almost
       A   **B**
    all fine-grained quartz specimens <u>may help</u> geologists pinpoint sites <u>holding</u> petroleum
              C   **D**
    deposits.

12. The jury <u>was instructed</u> to overlook <u>that</u> the accused had participated in several inflam-
        A   **B**
    matory rallies, and <u>that</u> he was on record as once having advocated the use of force in
          C
    the event of a government's attempt <u>to coerce</u> its citizenry.
                 D

13. In this culture, <u>having</u> five children <u>are considered</u> by many <u>to be</u> rather restricting,
         A   **B**   **C**
    though elsewhere <u>it is considered</u> a blessing.
          D

14. <u>Bent</u> over his desk, on hand still <u>clutching</u> a pencil, the student seemed <u>observing and</u>
    A   **B**   **C**
    <u>noting</u> things about some microscopic creature, but in reality he <u>had fallen asleep</u>.
                     D

15. <u>Given</u> <u>the fact that</u> they store every single document they have ever produced on the
     A **B**
    hard disk, <u>it was bound</u> <u>that</u> they would run out of memory eventually.
        C   **D**

16. <u>That</u> only Saturn had rings <u>it was presumed</u> <u>to be correct</u> until the transmissions of the
    A   **B**   **C**
    Voyager space probes <u>expanded our understanding</u> with startling new data from the
             D
    outer planets.

17. The suggestion <u>which</u> his aunt, the Archduchess Isabella, <u>intended to employ</u> the painter
          A   **B**

    Rubens on diplomatic missions initially filled King Phillip IV of Spain with doubt, a

    feeling <u>that</u> he soon altered <u>after meeting the man</u>.
        C   **D**

18. Sean assured his father that <u>if he were</u> with a group of friends <u>who had been drinking</u>,
                               A   **B**

    he would remind them <u>of that</u> none of them <u>should drive</u>.
                       C   **D**

19. The assistant manager's <u>recommendation</u> <u>that</u> the accountant <u>is fired</u> <u>was received</u> with
                           A   **B**   **C**   **D**

    little enthusiasm.

20. It <u>continues that</u> the notion <u>that</u> there are only three kingdoms in the natural world—
          A   **B**

    animal, vegetable, and mineral—though most biologists now <u>sort things into</u> five
                                                        C

    kingdoms, the fungi <u>having</u> one all to themselves.
                          D

UNIT 24

Emphasizing and Focusing Structures

Exercise 1 *(Focus 1)*

Use the cues in parentheses to add a phrase or clause to each sentence. To emphasize the description you added, move it to the front of the sentence. If you wish, you can add other descriptive words or phrases.

E X A M P L E : The creatures chased the mayor. (direction)
Down the long corridors of the city hall, the creatures chased the terrified mayor.

1. The creatures began moving.

    a. (time) _____.

    b. (manner) _____.

    c. (direction) _____.

2. The detective spoke with the victim's girlfriend.

    a. (purpose) _____.

    b. (position) _____.

    c. (manner) _____.

3. The group approached the great chest.

    a. (time) _____.

    b. (reason) _____.

    c. (manner) _____.

4. The scientists saw a city with large pyramids.

    a. (position) _____.

    b. (manner) _____.

    c. (time) _____.

5. Max will buy Ramona a diamond ring.

    a. (condition) _____.

    b. (reason) _____.

    c. (position) _____.

186

Exercise 2 *(Focus 2)*

Use an appropriate word or phrase from the list below to complete the blanks with fronted structures.

No sooner	Not for anything
Around me	Never
Almost never	Little did I realize
So weak	In the center of the village
Little did we suspect	Fluttering through the air
Not quite as bad as everyone feared	

(a) _____ that morning that I would wind up in a hospital room at night. My wife and I were home again after traveling in Asia for one year. It was a beautiful October day, crisp and clear, and the colors of the leaves were brilliant. We drove to one of our favorite villages. **(b)** _____ were hundreds of colorful leaves. We parked the car and got out with our cameras.
(c) _____ was a white wooden church. The scent of apples, crushed leaves, and harvested fields was in the air. **(d)** _____ would I have wanted to be anywhere else at that moment. All of a sudden I felt very dizzy. I made my way to the car and curled up in the back seat. I shivered as my wife drove, but by the time we reached home I was hot and sweating. **(e)** _____ had I been ill before, so I was completely bewildered by the waves of cold then heat that were passing over me. **(f)** _____ was I that I could barely climb up the stairs to the bedroom. I collapsed into bed, and after that I remember only strange snatches of feverish dreams until I came to in the hospital.
(g) _____ were the concerned faces of my wife and the hospital staff. They were glad to see me conscious again. I had been put in a private room because the doctors were worried I might have a contagious disease, caught in the course of my travels. During the night, the cold spells abated but the fever remained and I had to sleep with the window wide open and only one sheet. **(h)** _____ was the diagnosis the next day. I had a particularly virulent case of pneumonia. I was treated well and began to recover quickly, but twice daily for the next five days a nurse came to help me clear my lungs. **(i)** _____ have I been pounded so hard on the back.

My wife visited every day and brought with her books and good things to eat.

(j) _____ that the roles would quickly be reversed.

(k) _____ did I get home than she came down with the

same disease.

Exercise 3 *(Focus 3)*

Add a main clause after each of the following phrases, expressing your opinions or providing information. If the fronted constituent is a position adverb, use a *be* verb to follow it.

E X A M P L E :   Outside the administration building *is a famous piece of sculpture.*

1. Never in my life _____ .
2. More amazing than ever before _____ .
3. Seldom during this century _____ .
4. In the parking lot _____ .
5. More inspiring to me than anything _____ .
6. Rarely in my family _____ .
7. More of a health problem than obesity _____ .
8. So sad _____ that _____ .
9. Hidden away, unsuspected _____ .
10. Beckoning from the limousine _____ .
11. At the top of the Empire State Building _____ .
12. Better than Christmas _____ .
13. Hailed and honored as the genius of the century _____ .
14. So delightful _____ that _____ .

Exercise 4 *(Focus 4)*

Add the negative fronted structure in parentheses to the following sentences for emphasis. Make any other changes that are necessary.

E X A M P L E :   I will not eat brains. (not for any amount of money)
          Not for any amount of money will I eat brains.

1. That restaurant does not permit smoking. (under no conditions)

_____

2. He has never said sorry. (not once)

_____

3. I wouldn't take that drug. (not for anything)

_____

4. She hadn't ever felt so insulted. (never)

_____

5. The theater will not allow children to see that movie. (under no circumstances)

_____

6. I haven't gone swimming yet this year. None of my friends have. (neither)

_____

7. This does not alter my opinion. (in no way)

_____

8. They cannot leave the children unattended at home. (in no case)

_____

Exercise 5 (Focus 4)

Complete the following statements with information about yourself.

1. Nowhere _____

_____

2. Not until I finish my studies _____

_____

3. Not since I left _____

_____

4. Not until very recently _____

_____

5. No way _____

_____

6. Not since as long as I can remember _____

_____

Exercise 6 (*Focus 5*)

In the dialogue below, a group of friends are discussing the film they have just seen. Emphasize the negatives or implied negatives in each underlined statement by rephrasing the statement with a fronted negative. Make other changes as necessary.

E X A M P L E :   I have never seen such an action-packed film as *The Lost City of the Xinca.*
Never have I seen such an action-packed film as The Lost City of the Xinca.

Michiko: Wasn't that an exciting film? (1) I've hardly ever been on the edge of my seat as much.

Juan: I totally agree. Remember the part when they had to cross the river? (2) They had no sooner reached the middle when all these eyes and crooked smiles appeared on the surface.

Dmitri: Yeah. And how about the time the snake crawled into the leader's sleeping bag in the night? (3) She had hardly told the rest of the group that there was nothing to worry about because of the campfire when a huge boa constrictor crawled out of the brush.

Inga: (4) And the next morning, they had scarcely pulled the bald guy out of the quicksand when there was an earthquake. And out from the crack at their feet poured thousands of army ants. That really gave me the creeps.

Juan: And then they got captured in nets. It was all Clive's fault. (5) It was only because of his pig-headed insistence that they took the lower route. Too bad one of those horrible spiders didn't get him instead of Miss Albers.

Michiko: Absolutely. But he got what he deserved in the end. But before that they were all led into the city. (6) They didn't know why the people were giving them flowers and smiling at them. [begin with *Little . . .*]

Dmitri: (7) They realized what was really going on only later. Beginning with Clive they they were led up the steps of the pyramid.

Inga: (8) Professor Winbigler herself did not understand what was in store for them until she heard Clive's terrible scream.

Juan: Lucky for the rest of them that she found a couple of flares in one of her many pockets. (9) The remainder of the team survived only because of that lucky find.

Inga: They also survived because of the Xinca legend regarding a woman who would come one day with the power to make fire shoot from her hands. (10) Professor Winbigler had never in her wildest imagination thought she would be considered a divine messenger. I wonder how she adjusted to being an ordinary scientist again after they escaped.

Michiko: I'm sure that part was easy. (11) She would in no way want to be a priestess in that gruesome city.

Dmitri: That was certainly a great film. I might even go see it again. You know, it's too bad Ivan couldn't make it. (12) If he had known it was going to be so thrilling, he would definitely have come with us.

1. _____
2. _____
3. _____
4. _____
5. _____
6. _____
7. _____
8. _____
9. _____
10. _____
11. _____
12. _____

Exercise 7 *(Focus 6)*

State what you think is the main reason for fronting each of the underlined structures. Do you think it is primarily for (1) emphasis of the fronted structure, (2) contrast of the structure, or (3) focus on the delayed subject?

1. On Monday, I'm usually a little reluctant to get out of bed in the morning and begin another week of work. By Friday, the week's tasks nearly at an end, I usually spring right up when I hear the alarm ring.

2. Three quarters of what I get in the mail is either plain junk or charities asking for money. Imagine, then, my surprise yesterday on tearing open a letter to find ten crisp hundred dollar bills inside.

3. When I drive, rarely do I exceed the speed limit. I've never received a speeding ticket and I've never had an accident either.

4. Had you called someone you would have known the class was going to meet at a restaurant instead of at school. Why didn't you phone?

5. Professor Winbigler raised the lighted flares and closed her eyes because of the smoke and the sparks. When she heard a great hush and a rustling below, she chanced to open her eyes. Groveling at her feet was the high priest, the red dagger held up in his palms as an offering.

6. In the front of the building is an opulent marble facade facing a busy street. In the back, the trash bins line a narrow brick alley with fire escapes.

7. Not since before her illness did Alice remember how happy the sight of the sea had made her. After months of pain and struggle, she stood on the beach, with tears of joy running down her cheeks.

8. Rumors spread through the restaurant like wildfire. Everyone was soon more interested in the door than in what was on their plates. <u>And then, finally, unbelievably, framed in the entryway</u> was the President of the United States and the First Lady.

9. <u>Not until the bell rings</u> can anyone leave the room. You must all remain here until then, even if you've finished the exam.

10. <u>Only when his wife is on a business trip</u> does he do any housework. Normally, he doesn't seem to notice what happens to the dirty dishes.

Exercise 8 (Focus 6)

In each of these brief dialogues there is something wrong with the form of the statement or the use in context of the second speaker. Identify the problem. Correct errors in form and explain problems with usage.

1. **Receptionist:** A single room is $750 plus tax, not including breakfast.
   Tourist: I have nowhere been that is this expensive.

2. **Teacher:** Have you forgotten what we studied yesterday?
   Student: Scarcely had you mentioned it when I forgot.

3. **Flight attendant:** Is there something wrong with your chicken, sir?
   Airline traveler: Little do you know I am a vegetarian.

4. **Doctor:** What can I do for you today?
   Patient: You must help me, doctor. Never I have been in such pain before.

5. **Police Officer:** Do you know you were going 90 miles per hour? What's the rush?
   Motorist: No way am I going to be late for work.

6. **Doctor:** I would recommend a cortisone injection if you want to get rid of that condition quickly.
   Patient: Not under any circumstances I can take cortisone. I'm afraid I'm allergic to it.

UNIT
25

It as a Focusing Device

Exercise 1 *(Focus 1)*

The columns below consist of general knowledge information. Match the focus element with the appropriate clause and then make a complete sentence beginning with *It + be*, and linking the two elements with *that*, *who*, or *where*. Make any other necessary changes.

E X A M P L E :   *It was Florence that led the Renaissance in the arts.* (3-g)

1. Carl Jung
2. Chicago
3. Florence
4. Marco Polo
5. Versailles
6. the Wright Brothers
7. China
8. the Black Death
9. Wyoming
10. the Hajj

a. reached China during the rule of Kublai Khan.
b. made the first successful flight in a gasoline-powered aircraft.
c. is the pilgrimage to the holy city of Mecca during the twelfth month of the Islamic year.
d. the first book was printed.
e. developed the psychoanalytical theory of archetypes.
f. is the most rural state in the U.S.
g. led the Renaissance in the arts.
h. the treaty that ended World War I was signed.
i. the world's tallest building is located.
j. wiped out more than a third of Europe's population in the fourteenth century.

1. _____
2. _____
3. _____
4. _____
5. _____
6. _____
7. _____
8. _____
9. _____
10. _____

Exercise 2 *(Focus 2)*

Which person in your family or circle of friends best matches the following descriptions? Use a cleft sentence beginning with "it is" (or "it's") in your response.

E X A M P L E : *It's my sister-in-law Meg who* tends to send everyone a birthday card.

1. _____ is the most practical. (family member)

2. _____ tends to be a better listener than talker. (family member or friend)

3. _____ tends to like to stay up late at night. (family member or friend)

4. _____ has traveled to more countries than anyone else. (family member)

5. _____ would be most likely to clean up a messy room. (family member)

6. _____ tends to be well-informed about politics. (family member or friend)

7. _____ most enjoys eating. (family member or friend)

8. _____ is in the best physical condition. (family member or friend)

Exercise 3 *(Focus 2)*

Choose a word from the list for a focus element and complete each blank so that the sentence is a cleft construction. The first one has been done for you as an example.

inspiration	a drought
revenge	stagefright
stamina	memory

1. _____*It is revenge*_____ that often provokes a vicious circle in response to an initial wrongdoing.

2. _____ that enables an athlete to endure even when there is little energy left.

3. _____ that is tragically lost due to Alzheimer's disease.

4. _____ that prevented the award winner from giving a speech at the banquet.

5. _____ that accounts for a creative person's new ideas.

6. _____ that drove many to abandon their homes in Oklahoma and move to California in the 1930s.

Exercise 4 *(Focus 3)*

Restate the following sentences about the discoveries and events which led to the creation of the atom bomb to emphasize the information indicated in parentheses. Change any other wording as necessary. The first one has been done for you as an example.

1. Leo Szilard, a Hungarian physicist, who had left Nazi Germany, realized the possibility of setting up a nuclear chain reaction in 1933. (emphasize the date)
   It was in 1933 that Leo Szilard, a Hungarian physicist who had left Nazi Germany,

   realized the possibility of setting up a nuclear chain reaction.

2. In the winter of 1938, the German scientists Otto Hahn and Fritz Strassman demonstrated the process of nuclear fission. (emphasize the scientists)

   _____

   _____

3. In 1939 Albert Einstein wrote a letter to President Roosevelt to inform him about recent discoveries concerning uranium and also about the possibility of constructing a powerful bomb. (emphasize the purpose)

   _____

   _____

4. In August 1942, the top-secret Manhattan project was established to develop an explosive device based on nuclear fission. (emphasize the purpose)

   _____

   _____

5. On December 2, 1942, Enrico Fermi and his colleagues produced the first controlled nuclear reaction in a squash court beneath the stands of an abandoned football field at the University of Chicago. (emphasize the place)

   _____

   _____

6. In 1943 the Army chose J. Robert Oppenheimer to direct the lab in Los Alamos, New Mexico where the atomic bombs would be designed and assembled. (emphasize the director)

   _____

   _____

7. The uranium and plutonium for the bombs was produced by huge reactors and separator plants in Washington and Tennessee. (emphasize the production facilities)

   _____

   _____

8. The first atomic bomb was detonated near Alamogordo, New Mexico, on July 16, 1945. (emphasize the date)

_____

_____

Exercise 5 (*Focus 3*)

The following sentences explain either the causes or effects of an action. Use a cleft construction with the appropriate tense and either *out of* (reason) or *for* (purpose) plus a word from the list to complete them. The first one has been done for you as an example.

glory	frustration
malice	his country
generosity	a sense of honor

1. It is _____ *for glory* _____ that many rulers have set out to conquer.

2. It was _____ that many young men joined the army in World War I and not because they truly wished to fight.

3. It is _____ that many people donate large sums of money to charitable causes.

4. It was _____ that the gang of boys threw stones at the starving dog.

5. It was _____ that Nathan Hale, an American patriot hanged by the British, said he was giving his life.

6. It was _____ that the writer threw down his pen after sitting at his desk for an hour without having produced one interesting sentence.

Exercise 6 (*Focus 3*)

Imagine that each of the situations is true. Provide an explanation, either serious or humorous, emphasizing the reason. The first one has been done for you as an example.

1. Your mother didn't receive a phone call from you on Mother's Day.
   It's because the lines were busy that I couldn't get through.

2. You receive a notice from the library informing you of books overdue one month.

   _____

3. You didn't receive the grade you wished for on your last English exam.

   _____

4. Someone points out that you are wearing two socks of completely different styles.

_____

5. You can't make it to class today.

_____

6. A friend asks you why you were caught speeding.

_____

Exercise 7 (Focus 4)

You have been asked to edit a reference book manuscript for errors. Unfortunately, much of the book turns out to be a veritable treasury of misinformation. As you read each fact, identify the part that is incorrect. Make up a statement indicating to the author what needs to be corrected, using a cleft sentence to highlight that element.

E X A M P L E : Situated in the Andes range, K2 at 28,250 feet is the world's second highest peak.

Correction: _It is in the Karakoram range that K2 is situated._

1. Harrison Ford starred in the first six James Bond films.

_____

2. Zambia is the next country directly to the north of South Africa.

_____

3. The election of 1860 of an antislavery candidate, Thomas Jefferson, as President prompted seven southern states to break away from the Union, an action which led to civil war.

_____

4. The cerebrum makes up two-thirds of the entire heart and is divided into two interconnected halves, or hemispheres.

_____

5. _The Werewolf of London_ is a novel by Mary Shelley about a scientist who brings to life a hideous suffering creature without a sense of good and evil who finally kills his creator.

_____

6. Between 1519 and 1521, Francisco Pizarro conquered Mexico and ended the Aztec Empire.

_____

7. A person given a virus is made immune to the disease and cannot pass it on to anyone else.

_____

8. In 1445 Johann Gutenberg published the complete works of Shakespeare, the first printed book in Europe.

_____

9. The game of backgammon ends by checkmate, a term from the Persian "shah mat," which means the king is dead.

_____

Exercise 8 *(Focus 5)*

First, complete each list below with four examples:

FAVORITE PLACES

1. _____
2. _____
3. _____
4. _____

FAVORITE AUTHORS

1. _____
2. _____
3. _____
4. _____

FAVORITE FLOWERS

1. _____
2. _____
3. _____
4. _____

FAVORITE [YOUR CHOICE]

1. _____
2. _____
3. _____
4. _____

Now, to indicate which items rank highest from each of the first three lists, fill in the blanks of the sentences below. Share one or two of your responses with classmates.

1. I would love to be in _____ , _____ ,
   and _____ . But it is _____
   that I would chose to be in right now if I could be instantly transported there.

2. I enjoy _____ , _____ ,
   and _____ very much. But it is _____
   I would pick as the top of my list because I think of his/her works most frequently.

3. I love _____ , _____ ,
   and _____ . But it is _____
   I love best because _____ .

4. With the fourth list of your favorites, make up a sentence using the pattern above.

_____

_____

Exercise 9 *(Focus 6)*

Choose one feature to highlight among the following historical facts and write an introductory sentence for a historical narrative about each person.

E X A M P L E : *It was in 485* B.C. *that Cincinnatus took command and rescued the Roman army.*

Person	Date	Place	Event
Cincinnatus (leader)	485 B.C.	Rome	Takes command and rescues army surrounded by enemy
Mohammed (prophet)	622 A.D.	Arabia	Flees Mecca for Medina
Ashot I (ruler)	859 A.D.	Armenia	Founds Bagratide dynasty
Marco Polo (traveler)	1298 A.D.	Genoa	Begins to dictate his memoirs in jail
Francis Drake (explorer, pirate)	1581 A.D.	England	Returns from voyage of circumnavigation
Beethoven (composer)	1792 A.D.	Vienna	Becomes Haydn's pupil
Frank Whittle (inventor)	1937 A.D.	England	Builds first jet engine

Exercise 10 *(Focus 7)*

Make up a cleft sentence for each situation that follows. The first one has been done for you as an example.

1. You want to thank a friend for the great party that he gave last Saturday night.
   What a great party it was that you gave last Saturday!

2. You are busily taking notes in a Medicine class as the lecturer explains how gamma globulin types differ. Someone behind you has a brief coughing fit and you miss what he says. Politely ask the instructor to go over the last mentioned point.

3. Yesterday your spouse asked you when the insurance payment was due. You said it was on the 15th. Today your spouse asks you if it is due on the 16th. Tell him/her what you said.

4. The telephone rings very late at night and wakes you up. Someone in the house answers it. You wonder who could have been calling so late but you don't ask until the next morning.

_____

5. You are listening to the weather report on the radio with your grandfather, whose hearing is not so good. The meteorologist has just said that rain is on the way because of a low pressure front coming in from the south. Your grandfather wants to know why it's going to rain. You tell him what the meteorologist said.

_____

6. You are applying for financial aid at your college and an administrator gives you a form you've never seen before. You don't understand what you should fill out on the form. Ask her.

_____

Preposition Clusters

Exercise 1 (Focus 1)

The following sentences contain verb + preposition clusters. Complete them in two ways: with a noun phrase and with a gerund.

> E X A M P L E :   How could anyone object to a *low speed limit in a thickly settled neighborhood?*
> *reducing speed in an urban area?*

1. Only after I finish my work will I be able to think about _____
   _____.

2. The president commented on _____
   _____.

3. My parents do not approve of _____
   _____.

4. I'd hate to have to pay for _____
   _____.

5. All she ever does is talk about _____
   _____.

6. He assured me that he believed in _____
   _____.

7. Do you think she'll really consent to _____
   _____?

8. After weeks of research we finally decided on _____
   _____.

9. The leader warned the people not to rely on _____
   _____.

10. Is it true that you've been complaining about _____
    _____?

Exercise 2 (Focus 2)

Fill in the following blanks using verb + *at*. In some cases, more than one answer is possible.

EXAMPLE: After knocking his glass over and spilling the contents all over the table, the embarrassed guest sheepishly *grinned at* the hostess and apologized.

1. "I had so much work to do last night that I only _____ the opening pages of your report. From what I could see, it looked quite interesting."

2. "While you're draining the oil, would you mind _____ the front brakes too?"

3. The teacher _____ one of the exams that had just been turned in. It was creased, full of smudges and crossed out words, and had lines and arrows going everywhere.

4. The two burglars _____ each other when they found the door to the vault open.

5. The burly high school football player _____ his opponent in the line who was making disparaging remarks.

6. Obviously star-struck, the busload of tourists _____ the film celebrities leaving the studio.

Exercise 3 (Focus 3)

Select one word or phrase from the following three columns to create a question using verb + *with*.

EXAMPLE: *How can citizens cooperate with the police in the fight against crime?*

Column #1	Column #2	Column #3
Citizens	Undercover agent	To defeat a common foe
One side	Drug dealers	Before signing a deed
FBI	An attorney	In the fight against crime
Rock musicians	Inherited wealth	To benefit the entire natural community
Home buyer	Environmentalists	In their quest for inspiration
Talent	Police	In a sting operation
Developers	An old enemy	Produce success

1. _____

   _____

2. _____

_____

3. _____

_____

4. _____

_____

5. _____

_____

6. _____

_____

7. _____

_____

8. _____

_____

9. _____

_____

10. _____

_____

Exercise 4 *(Focus 4)*

Fill in one of the following verbs + *from* in each blank.

abstain	deviate	emerge	recede	separate
desist	differ	escape	recoil	shrink
detach	dissent	flee	retire	withdraw

1. According to the Hindu concept, there are four stages of life. The first stage is that of student. A student's chief obligation is to learn, and, as an apprentice, he is under the guidance of a teacher whom he must not (a) _____. The second stage, or physical prime of life beginning with marriage, is that of householder with its obligations to family and community. The third stage occurs when the person (b) _____ the busy world of work. Anytime after the arrival of the first grandchild, the individual may (c) _____ the social obligations he has shouldered in order to devote himself to philosophical inquiry and self-under-standing. The final stage is that of the "sannyasin," the wise man who has come to a

203

clear understanding of life and who is completely (d) _____ the strivings of the world. The sannyasin has no fixed abode, no belongings, no goal, no pride, and no expectations. Finally, he is free.

2. Heinrich Harrer was a German mountaineer who was captured by the British while on a climbing expedition in India at the beginning of the Second World War. His first two attempts to (a) _____ the camp he was confined in were failures. But on the third attempt he succeeded. (b) _____ his British and Indian pursuers, and then subsequently from bandits, he made his way through Tibet to the capital, Lhasa, where he eventually became a tutor of the current Dalai Lama.

3. The southern states (a) _____ the policies promulgated by Abraham Lincoln. As a result they decided (b) _____ the Union.

4. My cousin Ralph always felt he was a square peg in a round hole. With his strange hairstyles, outlandish dress, and outrageous opinions, he clearly (a) _____ the norm. Though he (b) _____ violence, he could never say no to the promises of pleasure which were typically in the forms of drugs and alcohol. He became an addict and total dropout and eventually many of his former friends wound up (c) _____ him. Fortunately, he found his way to a treatment center and began putting his life in order. When I saw him at a dinner last week, he told me he had been (d) _____ drugs and alcohol for a year and a half. I was impressed by how good and cheerful he looked and I wished him continued luck.

Exercise 5 *(Focus 5)*

Fill in the blanks with the appropriate verb + *for*. Try to use a different verb for each sentence.

E X A M P L E : Anyone who has lived under a repressive political system knows what it's like *to long for* freedom.

1. My mother is a very religious person and every day she _____ her family and world peace.

2. "I'm sorry, but this isn't what I ordered. I _____ apple pie, not chocolate cake."

3. There is a school of thought in contemporary psychology which maintains that an addict, on a very basic level, _____ wholeness.

204

4. My sister Joan, who is a runner, is presently sidelined with an injury, and she
_____ the day when she'll be able to run freely again.

5. It's interesting that when you are on a special diet, you _____ things
you shouldn't have, even if you didn't often eat them.

6. When I take an airplane, I usually _____ a window seat so I can see
the view.

7. Winter can seem very long to people who live in the northern tier of the United States.
Usually, sometime in February, people begin _____ Spring.

8. In the United States, it's customary for people to _____ something
on their birthday before blowing out the candles on their cake.

Exercise 6 *(Focus 6)*

Create your own questions for the following answers, using two different adjectives + preposition phrases from Focus 6.

EXAMPLE: A xenophobic pharmacist
   Who is *afraid of* foreigners and an *expert at* prescriptions and pills?

1. A nostalgic student
2. A newly arrived doctor
3. A secure accountant
4. An unprejudiced fireman
5. A paranoid jeweler
6. An enthusiastic grandmother
7. A humble linguist

1. _____
2. _____
3. _____
4. _____
5. _____
6. _____
7. _____

Exercise 7 (Focus 6)

Discuss what the following organizations are *interested in, concerned about, accustomed to, committed to, dedicated to, opposed to,* and/or *preoccupied with.*

E X A M P L E : *UNESCO is dedicated to developing education internationally and arranging scientific and cultural exchanges.*

1. World Wildlife Fund
2. Mothers Against Drunk Driving (MADD)
3. National Rifle Association (NRA)
4. CARE
5. The American Civil Liberties Union (ACLU)
6. The Sierra Club
7. The March of Dimes
8. The International Eye Foundation

1. _____

2. _____

3. _____

4. _____

5. _____

6. _____

7. _____

8. _____

Exercise 8 (Focus 7)

Write *in (the)* or *on (the)* in the following blanks.

E X A M P L E : *In the* event of rain, the picnic will be postponed to next Friday.

1. _____ advice of my physician, I regret to inform you that I shall have to resign my post.

2. They had to cancel school for the rest of the week _____ account of the bad weather.

3. All those _____ favor of the proposal, say "Aye."

4. _____ process of investigating the atom and nuclear reactions, scientists discovered subatomic particles.

5. Pull the red switch in the elevator only _____ case of emergency.

6. The Smiths have different ways of winding down after a day's work. He goes out jogging while she's _____ habit of sitting down and putting on the news.

7. _____ basis of economic necessity, the city council had to reduce the number of hours the library would stay open on weekends.

8. The teacher had to give William an "Incomplete" for the course. There were two major papers he didn't hand in, and his attendance was erratic. _____ top of everything else, he didn't show up for the final examination.

9. The department of Maintenance and Operations is _____ charge of a multitude of jobs, from repairing leaky pipes to running the campus post office.

Exercise 9 (Focus 7)

Fill in the following blanks with the expressions below. Compare your answers with those of your classmates.

By means of	On the strength of	With the exception of
In the name of	On account of	In the course of
in return for	at odds with	in the process of

1. _____ the continuous influx to and within America, the American people have been a perpetually changing mixture of diverse cultures.

2. _____ history, the character of the American people has been reworked and replenished in each generation. It has never existed in what could be called a definitive form.

3. _____ kidnapped Africans and dispossessed Native Americans, the history of American settlement from the beginning was the record of people in search of promises, or, as some have said, of "castles in the air."

4. _____ the tales both true and misleading that they had heard of extraordinary New World gifts for the taking, early settlers came eagerly to this country, their Promised Land.

5. Every group that has come has found the country occupied by people that arrived earlier. Each great wave of immigrants met resistance and found themselves in some way _____ the reigning establishment.

6. Early traders exchanged iron tools and pots, blankets, firearms, and whisky with the Native Americans _____ furs, but tragically, _____ this exchange, the Native Americans' independence and self-sufficiency eventually gave way.

7. _____ its language, the British left a lasting stamp on America.

8. The early Pilgrims in the Massachusetts Bay Colony began all legal contracts with the phrase, "_____ God, Amen."

Exercise 10 (*Focus 8*)

Complete the following sentences.

1. Speaking of food, _____
_____.

2. With respect to the computer, _____
_____.

3. According to a recent poll, _____
_____.

4. Based on the witnesses' testimonies, _____
_____.

5. Pertaining to your insurance policy, _____
_____.

6. According to the latest issue of _____
_____.

7. With respect to my grandparents, _____
_____.

8. Based on what I have discovered this year, _____
_____.

9. Speaking of sports, _____
_____.

10. Pertaining to viruses, _____
_____.

Choose the one word or phrase that best completes the sentence.

1. During the War of the Spanish Succession from 1701–1713, the English and the Dutch switched allegiance from Charles of Austria in order to _____ Philip of Spain so as to prevent the union of France and Spain.

   (A) deviate from
   (B) sneer at
   (C) side with
   (D) cooperate for

2. No sooner had the island finished cleaning up the debris from the last hurricane _____ another ferocious storm struck.

   (A) when only
   (B) and
   (C) then
   (D) than

3. _____ that he kicked his car.

   (A) It was for desperation
   (B) It was out of desperation
   (C) Out of desperation was it
   (D) For desperation was it

4. _____ taking Thursday off, I suggest we take Friday.

   (A) In place of
   (B) On grounds of
   (C) In lieu of
   (D) In the event of

5. _____ anyone know that the old woman on the park bench had once been a famous actress.

   (A) Little did
   (B) Rarely has
   (C) It was rare for
   (D) Not only does

6. _____ smile at the blunders of his youth and regard them as simple indiscretions.

   (A) Not for anything could he
   (B) Not for anything he could
   (C) He could not make any
   (D) Could he not make any

7. Juanita has never cut her hair, _____ she ever intend to.

   (A) doesn't
   (B) never will
   (C) not does
   (D) nor does

8. _____ her husband, who was abroad making a film, she accepted the award and thanked the committee.

    (A) On account of

    (B) On the strength of

    (C) On behalf of

    (D) On grounds of

9. _____ that I stayed up long past my usual bedtime to finish it.

    (A) The book was suspenseful

    (B) So suspenseful was the book

    (C) So suspenseful the book was

    (D) In suspense was I

10. The Speaker of the House frowned _____ the disrespectful comments he heard coming from the upstairs gallery.

    (A) about

    (B) from

    (C) against

    (D) at

Identify the <u>one</u> underlined word or phrase that must be changed in order for the sentence to be grammatically correct.

11. Had they <u>known</u> to what extent their discoveries <u>would be put</u> to negative uses,
            A   **B**
<u>doubtful it is</u> that some inventors <u>would have revealed</u> what they had learned.
    C   **D**

12. <u>Not until</u> the end of the third Punic War in 146 BC, <u>when Rome emerged victorious</u>
    A   **B**
over Carthage, <u>Rome could claim</u> to control the coast of North Africa in the region
               C
that is <u>now known</u> as the Maghreb.
    D

13. Every age <u>has had</u> its share of controversial writers and ideas, but <u>rarely</u> <u>there has been</u>
          A   **B**   **C**
as much stir created <u>as by</u> the appearance in 1859 of Charles Darwin's *On the Origin of*
               C
Species by Natural Selection.

14. <u>Better than</u> anyone <u>could have anticipated</u> <u>there was</u> the medal-winning performance of
    A   **B**   **C**
the figure skater, and <u>only a short while, too,</u> after a major injury.
              D

15. Despite using torture <u>on top of</u> solitary confinement, the prison authorities
                A
<u>did not succeed in</u> getting the political prisoner <u>to cooperate with</u> them and
    B   **C**
<u>to dissent against</u> the party he had helped to found.
    D

16. For centuries people wondered <u>why was it</u> that <u>there were</u> so many circles of standing
   A   **B**
stones scattered all over the British Isles and Brittany, that is, <u>until</u> the theories became
                                                                    C
current <u>that they were built</u> as astronomical and seasonal observatories.
         D

17. <u>What</u> a stunning job <u>is it</u> <u>they are doing</u> now <u>cleaning</u> all the stained glass windows of
   A   **B**   **C**   **D**
Chartres cathedral.

18. <u>According</u> a recent study of bird behavior done <u>in the course of</u> research by Lance Work-
   A   **B**
man, a Welsh animal psychologist from the University of Glamorgan, robins, like
humans, develop regional accents, and will <u>even</u> become vexed <u>in the event of</u> hearing
                                            C   **D**
songs by members of the same species who hail from different places.

19. I <u>don't have any idea</u> why she <u>doesn't want</u> to speak with us and <u>anyone else does neither</u>
   A   **B**   **C**
<u>as far as I know</u>.
   D

20. <u>While the British controlled India</u>, many families were <u>in the process of</u> summering
   A   **B**
in the cool hills, where they built bungalows, <u>laid out</u> gardens, and <u>escaped from</u>
                                                C   **D**
enervating heat of the lower elevations.